The Economy
of
Communion

The Economy of Communion

Toward a Multi-Dimensional Economic Culture

Edited by
Luigino Bruni

Translated by
Lorna Gold

New City Press
Hyde Park, New York

This book is dedicated to Siobhan, Connie, Art and Daniel,
who believed in the "utopia" of the Economy of Communion
and recently reached the Source of every communion.

Published in the United States by
New City Press, 202 Cardinal Rd., Hyde Park, NY 12538
www.newcitypress.com
© 2002 New City Press

Cover design by Nick Cianfarani

Translated by Lorna Gold from the original Italian
Economia di Comunione
© 1999 Città Nuova, Rome, Italy

ISBN 1-56548-178-X

Printed in Canada

✧ Contents

✧ Translator's Note

Lorna Gold

Translating this book on the unique experience of the Economy of Communion from Italian has been a challenging, but extremely engaging enterprise. As one translates, one becomes increasingly aware that language, like the economy, is bound up in culture. Far from being couched in a neutral "scientific" language, economic ideas and theories are bound up in anecdotes, which are in many respects specific to the culture in which they originated. In translating this book, therefore, I have sought as far as possible to respect the original text, but a degree of interpretation is inevitable. I hope that any deviations I have made from the original text in view of making it more accessible to an English readership do not detract from the ideas of the authors.

One note worth emphasizing is the choice of the words "Economy of Communion" over "Economy of Sharing" throughout this text. Over the past few years, both phrases have been in use within the English language, and I too had grappled with both phrases in the course of my research. For while the "Economy of Communion" does not immediately tell us anything in English (unless you are already familiar with Christian theology or certain schools of sociology), the phrase "Economy of Sharing" is too reductive and narrow to express the deeper nature of the phenomenon under examination. Through this book I have come to realize the depth and scope of the word *communion* as a cultural concept that is almost completely absent from the English language, except in religious circles. Even then, its meaning has often been reduced to the liturgical act and not the *communio,* a mutual participation, association, sharing, fellowship. Translating this book has convinced me of the urgency of re-introducing this "missing" word into everyday English. Perhaps this is will be one of the by-products of translating this book into English.

✧ Introduction

Luigino Bruni

"When I proposed the Economy of Communion, I certainly did not have a theory in mind. Nonetheless, I can see that it draws the attention of economists, sociologists, philosophers and scholars from other disciplines. While this new experience, and the ideas and categories that underpin it, are rooted in the spirituality of unity, these scholars find reasons to be interested in it that go beyond the Movement in which historically it developed."[1]

This is how Chiara Lubich ended her speech at the Catholic University of the Sacred Heart in Piacenza, Italy, after she had been given an honorary degree in Economics.

This book about the Economy of Communion is proof of that interest by social and economic scholars to which Chiara Lubich was referring. It follows the first special issue of *Nuova Umanitá* (No. 80/81) dedicated to the Economy of Communion, which came out seven years ago. That text, which introduced the Economy of Communion immediately after its launch and presented it in different ways, is still a reference point for reflection on the meaning of this experience.

Over the years the Economy of Communion has come a long way, above all, in an empirical sense. Chiara launched this project in 1991. Within a year there were already a dozen or so pioneering businesses. Now the Economy of Communion involves around seven hundred businesses throughout the world.

---

1. Chiara Lubich, "Lezione tenuta in occasione del conferimento della laurea *honoris causa* in economia," *Nuova Unmaintá* 21/1 121 (1999): 18

Cultural reflection has also progressed alongside the growth of businesses. The first to take up the challenge were young people: almost one hundred theses have already been defended or are currently being written. As well as contributing directly to our understanding of the Economy of Communion, these students have spread the word about this experience among their professors in different countries. If the Economy of Communion now has a place in the debates over how to regulate economic life and human growth, it is partly as a result of their commitment and their conviction that the dream of an Economy of Communion could become a reality. There is growing interest in the subject within the scientific community and the Economy of Communion has offered several scholars new insights that have a bearing on theoretical reflection: the papers in the second part of this book begin to show this in relation to the economic sciences.

The first three articles presented here are introductory in nature and form the main co-coordinating points for the rest of the book. The first paper is a talk given by of Chiara Lubich in Strasbourg in May 1999. It is a concise and clear summary of the cultural and spiritual background from which the Economy of Communion historically emerged, as well as a description of the characteristics of the Economy of Communion. It forms a constant reference point for the other papers. The second article is by the sociologist Vera Araújo, who focuses on the culture and anthropology that underpins the project. This is followed by an article by Alberto Ferrucci, the project's coordinator, reviewing the history of the Economy of Communion over the past seven years from the perspective of the entrepreneurs engaged in it.

In the articles that follow the authors speak about the Economy of Communion from within the academic world of the economic sciences, using the language of those disciplines. There is a degree of diversity in the approaches and areas studied. The areas range from management science (Hans Burckart) to business studies (Mario Molteni), and from the history of economic thought (Luigino Bruni) to political economy (Stefano Zamagni and Benedetto Gui).

These articles are, above all, an attempt to begin to articulate, in the language of the economic sciences, what the Economy of Communion is, what is specific about it, and how it relates to similar experiences. The youthful experience of the Economy of Communion is then scrutinized through the instruments of economic science, with the aim of giving rise to important questions, highlighting certain aspects and proposing solutions.

The main point that emerges, in different ways and to varying degrees, in these articles, is the need for economic science to widen its "lens," so as to understand and describe the peculiarities of the phenomenon of the Economy of Communion. Some authors, in particular, underline the need to rethink the fundamental categories of economic science, such as economic good, welfare, and economic rationality, so as to understand and accurately describe the action of businesses with "ideal motivations."

All the authors seem to agree that the Economy of Communion does not represent important innovations with regard to "different" or "alternative" forms of business enterprise, so much so that participation in the project does not require juridical modifications or the institutional approval of the business. The real reason for interest in these businesses derives from the fact that they are expressions of a kind of *economic action* which is imbued with a "culture of giving" and communion. It is a lifestyle which many people all over the world already seek to put into practice in their everyday life: from the choice of how and what to consume, to how to save and invest, to how to run a business. This style of economic action, when translated into the organization of production, expresses itself in the desire to bring together respect for those rules and norms which govern business life with other values, motivations and objectives which can be summed up in the phrase "a culture of communion in freedom."

From what follows, it will become clear that there are many kinds of existing organizations, not currently considered as part of the Economy of Communion, which have the potential to participate fully in the project. It would just take someone with imagination and the desire for communion to get involved. Examples of such organizations include communitarian forms of consumption, saving and non-monetary exchanges; publishing houses and art galleries committed to spreading cultural ideas and values in tune with the project; and cultural institutions which are financed at least in part by trusts or donations. All of these could arguably adopt the spirit and message of the Economy of Communion more readily in different cultural spheres.

It has to be said, however, that no matter how renewed and enriched the concepts of economic science are, they will never be able to comprehend a reality like the Economy of Communion in its entirety. A living reality can only be understood through *continuous recourse to real life experience* and, therefore, through visiting those businesses that are participating and by entering, at least a little, into the daily routine of these men and women, these business people and workers who are fully immersed in the world of business but have their hearts elsewhere, but not very far away. Rather than worrying too much about accounts or sales, which are clearly important, they seem to be concerned with the well-being of the people who are around them (colleagues, employees, clients, people in need who they sometimes do not know, and even their competitors). And equally important, they are concerned with safeguarding their human and spiritual motivation. These are the people whom the authors of the articles collected here have in front of them in their attempts to theorize.

Finally, I would like to say that the work presented here is the result of a lively, fruitful and frank exchange among those who participated in it. While respecting each one's different sensitivities and personal convictions, the process of writing this book has enabled our intellectual research to gradually become a way of friendship and "communion," a way that is open to other scholars (some of whom have become involved in the theoretical reflections on the Economy of Communion indirectly through discussions with the authors). This work of pen and ink—or rather bits and keyboard—would like to be a note in the concert, in the symphony which is comprised of all those who worked and continue to work in the most diverse circumstances for the building of an economy which will really be "on a human scale."

✧ The Experience of the "Economy of Communion": A Proposal of Economic Action from the Spirituality of Unity

Chiara Lubich
Founder and President of the Focolare Movement

Strasbourg, France 31 May 1999
Parliamentary Assembly of the Council of Europe

Ladies and Gentlemen,

Thank you for inviting me to this important meeting to present to you a kind of economic action which is most fully expressed in the "Economy of Communion" project. This project is a particular experience of social economy, which has developed within the realms of the Focolare Movement.

I am not an economist, and the first part of my presentation, in particular, will not be of an economic nature. It may even seem strange to that field and to the language of economic science.

I will turn my attention to the Economy of Communion project in the second part of my talk.

It is certainly not new to affirm that every concept of economic life is the result of a particular culture and a precise vision of the world. Please allow me, therefore, to briefly tell you something about the ideal soil from which this type of economic action has emerged.

Over the past few decades, a lifestyle, which is the expression of a new culture, has been silently spreading in many nations. This culture, which is practiced above all in the Focolare

Movement, is Christian in origin and is animated by a new spirituality that is both personal and collective: the spirituality of unity. It has spread among people of all ages, races, languages, cultures and faiths. Among these, the vast majority are Catholics, but there are also people from the main world religions and others who do not share a particular religious reference point but share many values with us. This ecclesial reality has even begun to offer a new way of participating in the various fields of social life: from the field of politics to the world of culture, from the world of art to the economy, and so on.

The world vision of this movement is centered on the reality of God who is the Father of all. It follows that if God is Father, then all people are called to live as sons and daughters of God and, hence, as brothers and sisters in universal brotherhood, the foretaste of a more united world.

To bring this about it asks that each person put into practice in a decisive way what in religious terms is called Christian love, or benevolence for those of other faiths. In reality, this means desiring the good of the others, an attitude that is present in all sacred books. The idea of benevolence is not absent in so-called secular people either. Since every person is made in the image of God, who is one and three, all people have this model of the Creator within them, expressed in the instinct to enter into a relationship with others.

Every person, in fact, despite his or her weaknesses, finds it natural to adopt a culture that emphasizes giving rather than having, since each person is called to love other people.

Within the Focolare Movement it is precisely this "culture of giving," which has been quite distinctive right from the beginning, that gave rise not only to a communion of goods among all its members but to well-established social projects as well.

Love or benevolence, moreover, when lived out by two or more people, becomes reciprocal and gives rise to solidarity. Solidarity can only be kept alive through silencing one's own egoism, through facing difficulties and knowing how to overcome them.

The daily practice of this solidarity is the foundation of every action, also economic action, for the four and a half million people of the Focolare Movement and many people outside it.

It is a lifestyle which gives rise to a new way of doing politics. I will say a few words about this. Several years ago, in Italy, the Focolare gave rise what has been called the "Movement for Unity." Through this movement, politicians are asked to put reciprocal love into practice as the foundation of everything else. They remain within their existing political parties where they try to bring about unity. It means acting first—whether believers in God or not—as true believers in profound, eternal human values; and only then as defenders of their parties. What emerges is not a new political party encompassing everyone, but rather a situation in which the diversity of the other becomes an indispensable source of richness. This movement, which spread rapidly throughout Italy, has now spread to politicians in other European nations and beyond, based on the principle of "loving the other's country as your own." It is already beginning to show results both on a parliamentary level and in cities big and small.

Now we come to the economic dimension.

After fifty years, this lifestyle has given rise to the "Economy of Communion" project.

In May 1991, the Economy of Communion emerged during a meeting I had with the Focolare community of Sao Paolo, Brazil, the heart of a country that suffers in a dramatic way from the gulf between a wealthy minority and millions of very poor people.

Poverty had also appeared among several thousand of the 250,000 people who participate in our Movement in Brazil, making us realize that the communion of goods, which was already practiced, was no longer enough. It was then that the idea came to increase the communion of goods through giving rise to businesses, which would be entrusted to competent people who would be able to run them efficiently so as to make a profit.

One part of these profits would be used to help the business grow; a second part would be used to help those who are in need, giving them the possibility of living a dignified life while looking for work or through offering them work in the business itself. Finally, a third part would be used to develop educational structures for the formation of men and women motivated by a "culture of giving": "new people," since without new people it is not possible to build a new society.

The Economy of Communion was taken up with enthusiasm not only in Brazil and Latin America, but also in Europe and other parts of the world. It gave rise to many new businesses, and many existing ones also participated in the project through modifying the way that they run their business.

There are currently 654 businesses and ninety-one minor productive activities involved in the project.

The businesses involved are from a wide range of economic sectors in more than thirty countries. I will give you a few examples.

1. Prodiet Pharmaceutics, based in Curitiba, Brazil, has expanded from four to fifty employees and has increased its turnover fiftyfold over the past few years. It has now opened a subsidiary alongside five other Economy of Communion businesses in the industrial park created near Araceli, one of the model towns of the Movement in the region of Sao Paulo.

2. In the Philippine rural bank "Kabayan," the majority of the shareholders participate in the Economy of Communion. The bank, which is assisted by a consultancy firm also participating in the project, has moved from being the 123rd to the third largest rural bank in the Philippines in terms of deposits. It has opened eight branches with 150 collaborators. It managed to survive the Asian financial crisis of 1998 thanks to the trust created within and around the business.

3. Twenty-three business people from Solingen in Germany have set up a development investment fund called "Solidar Capital," which aims to promote the set-up and growth of new productive activities in Eastern European countries, the Middle East and Latin America.

4. The desire to participate in the Economy of Communion gave rise to the "Roberto Tassano Social Cooperatives Consortium" in Liguria, northern Italy. This consortium is now responsible for the management of a number of homes for the elderly, community homes for people with mental illness, and protective structures for people with special needs linked to industries in the local area. Over the past few years, the consortium has grown from a small initiative with a few founding members to 420 shareholders and has been defined as an "enterprise incubator" due to its capacity to give rise to new productive activities.

The experience of the Economy of Communion, with its peculiarities originating from the lifestyle that gave rise to it, sits alongside the numerous individual and collective efforts of those who have tried and are trying to "humanize" the economy. Some of these initiatives were also presented in this conference. The Economy of Communion businesses are committed, in every aspect of their activities, to putting the needs and aspirations of the human person, and the common good, at the center of their attention.

The businesses that participate in the Economy of Communion project operate within the market and to all intents and purposes are commercial firms or societies like any other. At the same time, however, these businesses propose something different. For them, the true meaning of all their economic activities lies not in the economic transaction *per se*, but in making it a "meeting place" in the deepest sense of the word: a place of communion. It is a place of communion, therefore, between those who have economic means and those who do not, communion between all those who are engaged in the economic activity in different forms. If it is true that the economy itself often contributes to creating barriers between social classes and different interest groups, these businesses seek to counter this in several ways. Firstly, they set aside part of their profits to provide urgent help to those who are in difficult economic situations. Secondly, within the businesses, relationships based on openness and trust among all those with a stake in the business—consumers, competitors, local and international community, public administration—are promoted, always bearing in mind the wider interests of all. Finally, these businesses undertake to put into practice and spread the culture of *giving*, of *peace*, of *lawfulness* and of respect for the *environment* (recognizing the need for solidarity with creation) both within and outside the business.

Here are a few characteristics of the Economy of Communion that are very significant for us because they are directly related to our vision of the world.

1. The actors within the Economy of Communion businesses seek to live out, in the particular way that their productive organization requires, the same lifestyle that they live in the other areas of their life.

2. The Economy of Communion businesses seek to apply behaviors inspired by selfless giving, solidarity and attention to the least not only within not-for-profit activities, but, mainly, within those businesses in which it is normal to seek profit. The profit is then shared within the perspective of communion.

3. The Economy of Communion businesses, while relying on the deep understanding that exists between the promoters of each business, feel that they are part of something bigger, in which an experience of communion is already being lived. They have developed within small (for the time

being at least) industrial parks near the twenty or so model towns of the Movement throughout the world or, if they are geographically distant, ideally they are "linked" to these towns in some way.

4. Those in economic difficulties who are helped by part of the profits are not considered as "assisted" by or "beneficiaries" of the business. They are regarded as essential active members of the project, within which they give their needs. They also live the culture of giving. In fact, many of them renounce the help they received just as soon as they have the bare minimum of economic independence. Others share what they have with those who are more in need.

5. Within the Economy of Communion the emphasis is not on the philanthropy of one or other, but rather on sharing, where each one gives and receives with equal dignity.

Many have asked how businesses like this, which are so attentive to the needs of everyone who comes into contact with the business and the needs of society at large, can survive within the market.

Certainly, the spirit that animates them also helps them to overcome the internal divisions that can sometimes be an obstacle and can even paralyze human organizations. Moreover, their way of operating attracts the trust and benevolence of clients, suppliers and financiers.

Nevertheless, it is important not to forget another indispensable element that has continuously accompanied the Economy of Communion over the years. These businesses leave room for God's intervention, even in concrete economic operations. After every choice to go against the current, which current business practice would discourage, God never fails to provide that "something more" which Christ promised: revenue which was unexpected, a new opportunity, the offer of collaboration, an idea for a new successful product.

This, in short, is the Economy of Communion. When I proposed it I certainly did not have a theory in mind. Nonetheless, I can see that it draws the attention of economists, sociologists, philosophers, and scholars from other disciplines. While this new experience, and the ideas and categories that underpin it, are rooted in the spirituality of unity, these scholars find reasons to be interested in it that go beyond the Movement in which historically it developed. In particular, within the category of "communion" some can see a new key to understand social relationships, which could help people get beyond the imposition of individualism that prevails within economic science today.

Distinguished ladies and gentlemen, this is my small contribution to this illustrious conference. I thank you for listening.

✧ Personal and Societal Prerequisites of the Economy of Communion

Vera Araùjo
International Cultural Institute "Mistici Corporis"
Loppiano, Incisa Valdarno, Italy

In the last decade before the turn of the millennium, the theme of "development" came sharply into relief in the debates surrounding global economic growth and globalization. This interest and general concern was highlighted in a series of international summits: *Environment and Development* in Rio de Janeiro, *Population and Development* in Cairo, *Women and Development* in Peking and *Social Development* in Copenhagen. A general conclusion emerged from all of these conferences: development is at the center of economic life; it is the goal of economic action and is the objective of economic activities.

Almost in parallel, within economic theory in the United States, highly esteemed economists—such as the Indian economist, Amartya Sen, who won the Nobel prize in 1988—came up with a new concept of development, known as "human development." This idea overcomes the concept of development which was linked only to economic growth and focuses on people, on their needs and some basic parameters which regard the quality of life: health, life span, education and degree of participation in social life.[1]

Human development is understood as the capability to exercise three essential possibilities: a long and healthy life, education, and access to the necessary resources to reach and maintain a dignified life.[2] It is now regarded as the goal and main objective

---

1. To these indicators one can also add other variables: the social, political and economic opportunities which exist to make use of creativity and one's spirit of initiative; full participation in social life; the sense of belonging to a community, and so on.
2. "Sen replaces the traditional concept of *welfare* with that of *well-being*, whose level consequently depends on several *functionings*. Taken together, these functionings

of all the measures of economic policy in official reports[3] and beyond.

These theoretical and technical lines, which have been offered to economic action, however, are in conflict with the economic policies used by large agencies and global economic institutions in various countries. Within these organizations, the dominant economic practices and ways of understanding the goals and objectives of economic action are going in exactly the opposite direction. They privilege the radical affirmation of the individual as an agent, leading to policies dominated by unfettered consumption that have disastrous consequences not only for human communities but for the environment and ecosystem too.

Such considerations convince us that if this problem is to be faced effectively we will have to dig much deeper to find the answers. We need to understand how the idea of human development itself emerges from a new anthropological concept. This concept emerges from the idea of *new persons* who are capable of surpassing their *modern* identities as producers and consumers, and finding *something extra* which will help them to open up to others and to liberate them from isolation and egoism. There is a need for a kind of person who could be called *homo donator,* who is capable of giving rise to the category of *gift* or sharing within public activities and, in particular, within economic ones. Only in this way will it be possible to see the outline of a new culture that expresses a vision of people and society in keeping with the aspirations, desires, wants and needs of this historical moment.

This culture can be called the *culture of giving.* It is not about being generous or benevolent or practicing philanthropy, nor is it about embracing the cause of charity. Rather, it is about learning and living out the dimension of gift, and giving oneself as an integral part of human existence.

---

make up the fulfillment of human *capabilities.* The capacity to benefit from the use of goods, and therefore to acquire functionings is closely conditioned by the effective use of these same goods." R. Targenti, "From Economic Development to Human Development," *Aggiornamenti Sociali* 11 (1997): 783.

3. Cf. United Nations Development Program (UNDP), *Human Development Report* (Turin, Italy, 1992).

The culture of giving encapsulates both the essence of the human person (by putting this relationship at the center and goal of everything) and a whole series of attitudes and behaviors that characterize human relationships.[4]

In other words, the culture of giving is about the nature of the human person as a being who is open to communion, to a relationship with the Absolute-God, with the others and with creation.[5] Individuality and sociality come together in the gift of self, in the gift of one's being and in the circulation of material and spiritual goods that are necessary for development, for growth and the maturity of all.

Not every kind of *giving*, however, results in the culture of giving.

There is a kind of "giving" which is tainted by the desire for power. It is an act that is full of the desire of domination, if not total oppression of individuals and peoples. This apparent "giving" is not really giving at all.

Then there is a kind of "giving" which seeks satisfaction and pleasure in the act of giving itself. This kind of giving is full of vanity, boastfulness, and is an expression of egoism and personality worship. In these situations, those who are on the receiving end see this act of giving as a humiliation or an offence.

Then there is a kind of utilitarian "giving" which has an ulterior motive and seeks a return, a profit. In some ways this is the kind of giving which is present in the current economic system

---

4. "Being is love, is relationship. The gift of one's self, therefore, is to be and, if well understood, is to be lost in every other person, but so as to be reborn, in order to 'be.' The internal dynamic of love is the stability and the permanence of being. Dynamics and stability are hence no longer mutually exclusive, but neither are they linked to each other simply through a dialectical mediation. Rather, in an indissoluble way, they are both unique and at the same time expressions of the 'God' event, the 'being' event, and the 'human' event." Klaus Hemmerle, *Partire dall'unità. La Trinità come stile di vita e forma di pensiero*, (Rome, Italy: Città Nuova, 1998), 45–46.

5. "Our personal being is assumed into the communion of life and love between the Father, Son and Spirit; in this way I can no longer represent the point of departure, the center and the point of arrival of my being in isolation. The Trinitarian existence can only be lived in reciprocity, as a 'we,' which at the same time does not dissolve I and you but constitutes them." Hemmerle, *Partire dall'unitá*, 45.

Finally, there is a kind of giving which Christians call *evangelical giving*.[6] This kind of giving unleashes a whole series of values that define the very act of giving as gratuity,[7] joy,[8] generosity, abundance,[9] and disinterest, thus removing the risks and dangers of being misunderstood or exploited.

The culture of giving is translated into action through the *art of giving*, in which all human relationships, lived out as a continuous and mutual self-giving, are oriented toward communion, which is synonymous with unity. In other words, the acts of giving, of sharing spiritual and material goods, are directed toward communion.[10] These relationships tend to become

6. Chiara Lubich asked: "What is this culture of giving? It is the culture of the gospel; it is the gospel, because we understood giving from the gospel. 'Give and gifts will be given to you, a good measure, packed together, shaken down, and overflowing, will be poured into your lap' (Lk 6:38). This is what we experience every day." Chiara Lubich, "Date e vi sará dato," *Economia di Comunione* 6 (April–July 1997): 3.

7. "You received without charge, give without charge." (Mt 10, 8).

8. "There is more happiness in giving than in receiving." (Acts 20, 35).

9. "Moreover, God has the power to give you an abundance of every grace so that, in this way, possessing all that you need, you can generously carry out all the good works. As it is written: 'He was rich, but he became poor for your sake, to make you rich out of his poverty' (2 Cor 8, 8–9). Clement of Alexandria comments: 'In this way, it is not he who has and who hoards up his gold who is rich, but rather, the one who distributes generously. It is not possessions that lead to happiness, but participating with the others.'" M. G. Mara, ed., *Richezza e povertá nel cristianesimo primitivo* (Rome, Italy: Città Nuova, 1980) 128.

10. "Our reciprocal relationship is not only about being courteous toward each other, but means having everything in common with the others; fundamentally this means living one, indivisible life. In an absolute sense, this is only true about God who is both the singular and indivisible substance, and at the same time a 'plurality' of persons. This is expressed and takes on a personal form in the gift of self—*donum*—in the Holy Spirit. . . . Nevertheless, this inter-divine substance also takes on a normative measure and is articulated in the rhythm of our life as participation in the life of God. This 'being one' that comes to light here has to be translated into something concrete. We can therefore only live in a Trinitarian way if this also reaches our wallet, both in terms of spiritual and material wealth. This means learning to put in common the goods of God and the goods of the world; it means treating others in such a way as not to just give them alms, but to really share with them. It is not about leveling out personal participation with regard to work or goods, since this is part of what brings joy and guarantees life for everything, for everyone. What is my own personally gives form to everything, lives off everything and places its imprint on everything. Our life is my life, our goods and my goods are no longer opposites which are mutually exclusive, but are realities which are contained within each other and leave a mark on each other." Hemmerle, *Partire dall'unitá*, 39–40.

reciprocal and mutual. Communion or unity comes about as a consequence. The society that derives from this is structured around communion since communion is the very essence of society and the individual person.

It is obvious that this type of society is in stark contrast with society today. The changes which came about through modernity opened wide the doors to individualism, egoism and an excessive search for one's self interest. This aspect of the human person, which has been lived out and pursued in every possible aspect of social life, has given rise to a *culture of having*, which now dominates our behavior.

I do not intend to reject or despise the aspect of having, but, as John Paul II says: "To 'have' objects and goods does not in itself perfect the human subject, unless it contributes to the maturing and enrichment of that subject's 'being,' that is to say, unless it contributes to the realization of the human vocation as such."[11] Further on he writes: "The evil does not consist in 'having' as such, but in possessing without regard for the quality and the ordered hierarchy of the goods one has. Quality and hierarchy arise from the subordination of goods and their availability to man's 'being' and his true vocation."[12]

Individualistic man has created a consumerist society[13] that dominates the whole of his existence.[14]

---

11. John Paul II, Encyclical Letter *Sollicitudo Rei Socialis* (Boston, MA: St. Paul Book & Media, 1987), 28.

12. John Paul II, Encyclical Letter *Sollicitudo Rei Socialis*, 28.

13. "This is the so-called civilization of 'consumption' or 'consumerism,' which involves so much 'throwing-away' and 'waste.' An object already owned but now superseded by something better is discarded, with no thought of its possible lasting value in itself, or of some other human being who is poorer. All of us experience firsthand the sad effects of this blind submission to pure consumerism: in the first place a crass materialism, and at the same time a radical dissatisfaction, because one quickly learns, unless one is shielded from the flood of publicity and the ceaseless and tempting offers of products, that the more one possesses the more one wants, while deeper aspirations remain unsatisfied and perhaps even stifled." John Paul II, Encyclical Letter *Sollicitudo Rei Socialis, 28.*

14. "Here we find a new limit on the market: there are collective and qualitative needs which cannot be satisfied by market mechanisms. There are important human needs that escape its logic. There are goods that by their very nature cannot and must not be bought or sold. Certainly the mechanisms of the market offer secure advantages: they help to utilize resources better; they promote the

Hence modern society is characterized as complex,[15] conflictual, alienating,[16] wasteful, joyful and sad, and above all, disillusioned. It is incapable of creating profound and durable relationships, since each one is locked in their own solitude.

The consequences are well known.

From an anthropological viewpoint, it leads to the domination of *homo consumens*[17]—the protagonist of a culture of having, eager to consume and incapable of subjective and moral consciousness.

From a political and social viewpoint, it leads to the spread of an aggressive competitiveness, feeding every kind of conflict and war, from those peoples and states to those conflicts that are perpetrated within the market and in the world of work.

Lets now reconsider the idea of communion.

---

exchange of products; above all they give central place to the person's desires and preferences, which, in a contract, meet the desires and preferences of another person. Nevertheless, these mechanisms carry the risk of an 'idolatry' of the market, an idolatry which ignores the existence of goods which by their nature are not and cannot be mere commodities." John Paul II, Encyclical Letter *Centesimus Annus* (Boston, MA: St. Paul Book & Media, 1991), 40.

15. Cf AA.VV., *La societá complessa,* Bologna, 1983, especially p. 237 and Domenico Fisichella, *Dilemmi della modernitá nel pensiero sociale* (Bologna, Italy: Il Mulino, 1993).

16. "The alienation which we find in modern society is almost total; it permeates man's relationship with his work, with the things he consumes, with the state, with his neighbors, and with himself. Man has created a world of things made by him unlike any that has existed before. He has constructed a complex social machine to administer the technical machine that he has created. But all of this construction threatens him. He does not feel that he is at the center and creator, but like a slave of the Golem that he has built. The greater the forces that he unleashes, the more he feels powerless as a human being. He finds a reflection of his power embodied in the things he has created, from which he feels alienated. He is dominated by what he has created and has lost a sense of ownership of himself. He has built a golden calf and says: 'These are your gods which brought you out of Egypt.' " Erich Fromm *Psicanalisi della societá contemporanea* (Milan, Italy: Mondadori, 1971), 125. See also John Paul II, *Centesimus Annus,* 41.

17. "A very large proportion of men and women living in those countries which are materially wealthy seem to have changed the *homo sapiens* species into *homo consumens*. From our earliest years we are molded into consumers, at the hands of publicity that is now like the air that we breathe. Once formed, this *homo consumens* and the publicity in turn influence the economy, creating and justifying ever greater needs: surplus becomes convenient, what is convenient becomes necessary, and what is necessary becomes indispensable." Pedro Arrupe, *Impegno cristiano per la guistizia* (Milan, Italy, 1981), 134.

Communion is a polyvalent reality. Above all, it is something religious and spiritual, since its source is God—the Trinity, communion of love between Persons, and in Christ who is the revelation of this mystery.[18]

Chiara Lubich, the inspiration behind a movement and a spirituality of unity, writes: "I felt that I was created as a gift for the person next to me, and the person next to me was created by God as a gift for me. As the Father in the Trinity is everything for the Son and the Son is everything for the Father."[19]

Trinitarian communion, therefore, as both substance and life, is the ontological foundation of every form of communion.[20]

But communion is also a sociological category, which the Russian sociologist George Gurvitch explained as "the manifestation of real sociality." He analyses the category of "communion" on a scale of intensity until the point of fusion as "us."[21]

---

18. *Sollicitudo rei socialis* affirms: "In the light of faith . . . the awareness of the common fatherhood of God, of the brotherhood of all in Christ, 'children in the Son,' and of the presence and life-giving action of the Holy Spirit will bring to our vision of the world a new criterion for interpreting it. Beyond human and natural bonds, already so close and strong, there is discerned in the light of faith a new model of the unity of the human race, which must ultimately inspire our solidarity. This supreme model of unity, which is a reflection of the intimate life of God, one God in three persons, is what we Christians mean by the word 'communion.' " John Paul II, Encyclical Letter *Sollicitudo Rei Socialis*, 40.

19. Chiara Lubich *Writings* September 2, 1949, in Judith Polivus, *United in His Name—Jesus in our Midst in the Experience and Thought of Chiara Lubich* (New York: New City Press, 1981), 67.

20. This doctrine emerges forcefully from the charism and life of Chiara Lubich. As Marisa Cerini confirmed, "In such a discussion, a conception of reality can be viewed through the primary place given, not to substance, but to the person, which is considered essentially in the relationship of giving and receiving. It is a conception, therefore, that is molded on intra-trinitarian love, and reveals in love the fundamental basis and deepest meaning of being. This is the idea that arises from Chiara's experience. By incorporating herself into the dynamism of the same divine self-giving—'into the movement of love which is God himself'—Chiara, in her turn, gives herself completely, in the totality of her being and in her relationship with others. This entire reality, then, reveals itself to Chiara with that trinitarian mark which constitutes her own being and inner life, opening up for her new avenues toward an ever more profound understanding of the trinitarian mystery." Marisa Cerini, *God Who Is Love—In the Experience and Thought of Chiara Lubich* (New York: New City Press, 1992), 53.

21. For Gurvitch " 'We' (like the 'French we,' 'the militant union we,' 'we parents') is a whole which is an irreducible plurality of its members, a new unbreakable unity, in which the whole tends to be immanent within the parts and the parts in

"Reciprocal immanence between [the] self, the others and us finds its apex"[22] in communion. Moreover, "those who participate in Communion feel like they are lifted up by a liberating breeze which eliminates all obstacles, freed from themselves and all the other social ties which could be a hindrance to them."[23]

The concept of communion that Gurvitch[24] puts forward is not the same as the Christian concept,[25] which is at the basis of the Economy of Communion. The relationship between the Self and Others, as he intends, is not communal in a Trinitarian sense. Nevertheless, his concept is an interesting and stimulating one to compare.

A communal society, which is inspired and modeled according to the Trinity of God, is not only an abstraction nor merely an aspiration. It is necessary for a renewed discovery of the Trinity as the principle and source of a new society. This entails, in the first instance, recognizing communion (or unity) as a paradigm which can generate new ways of reading, understanding and interpreting social realities—elucidating a new theory that is capable of comprehending those new relationships

---

the whole. This reciprocal immanence, which could also be defined as reciprocal participation of plurality in unity and unity in plurality, can take on different forms in the different 'We's.' " George Gurvitch, *La vocazione attuale della sociologia* (Bologna, Italy: Il Mulino, 1965), 165.

22. Gurvitch, *La vocazione attuale,* 207.

23. Gurvitch, *La vocazione attuale.*

24. "Communion is the highest step in the scale of participation, in the forces of attraction, in the depth of fusion as 'Us.' The members do not feel the least sense of pressure. They treat each other as 'us' in the deepest sense, and they gain a sense of 'liberation' from every social or individual weight. Communion presupposes full, total participation holding nothing back from 'us.' " Gurvitch, *La vocazione attuale.*

25. The Second Vatican Council highlights the analogy between human living together and the Trinitarian relationship as a life of communion: "The Lord Jesus, when praying to the Father 'that they may all be one . . . even as we are one' (Jn 17:21–22), has opened up new horizons closed to human reason by implying that there is a certain parallel between the union existing among the divine persons and the union of God's children in truth and love. It follows, then, that if human beings are the only creatures on earth that God has wanted for their own sake, they can fully discover their true selves only in a sincere self-giving." Second Vatican Ecumenical Council, Pastoral Constitution on the Church in the World of Today *Gaudium et Spes* (Collegeville, IN: The Liturgical Press), 24 (with adjustments for inclusive language).

and relations which come about in society. To use this paradigm as the source of a new society in reaching a new direction in our complex history, one has to recognize relationships as the defining characteristic on every level—interpersonal, social, systematic, structural and institutional.[26] Unity, therefore, is needed to constitute the *diversity*, every kind of diversity. It is needed to cement the *pluralism* that is recognized as a good and a source of wealth. It is needed to increase *participation* as the motor of social life. It is needed to give strength to *freedom* as an expression of human maturity. It is needed to breathe life into the *social praxis* at every level or dimension: from human rights to the economy; from justice to health; from art to the means of communication; from culture to respect for the environment, and so on.

In the Economy of Communion, communion can rise to the status of an *economic category*.

It is the businesses themselves—with their internal structures and organizations, as well as the economic actors that work within and around them—that are called and invited to create communion.

In this way, communion is not only possible within interpersonal and social relationships, but becomes the overbearing feature, even a right, within economic realities and structures.

It is not a utopia or wishful thinking. It has emerged from the recognition of the urgent need for a profound change in the economy as an important expression of human life. The search for an ever more "civilized" society, which is participative, harmonious, and creating the conditions for happiness and

---

26. "To confess the Trinity does not mean simply recognizing it as a principle, but accepting it as the fundamental model of our life. When we affirm and respect the diversity and pluralism amongst human beings, in fact we are confessing the Trinitarian distinction in persons. When distances are eliminated and we work together to bring about the equality between man and woman, between the lucky and the unlucky, between those near and far, in practice we are affirming the equality of the persons of the Trinity. When we make the effort to be 'one heart and soul' and learn to share everything, so that no one is in need, we are confessing the one God and welcoming the Trinitarian life within us" The Bishops of Navarra and the Basque Country, *Creer hoy en el Dios de Jesu Cristo,* Easter 1986, in Enrico Cambon *Trinità modello sociale* (Rome, Italy: Città Nuova, 1999), 9.

well-being of individuals, communities and peoples demands that we go beyond a conflictual, aggressive and alienating economy in which competition has no limits. The voices of those calling for greater solidarity, integration, interaction, dialogue and the ability to listen to different viewpoints are getting louder. This goes to show the relevance of the Economy of Communion as an advanced point of an alternative economy to the one that dominates today.

In conclusion, it could be said that, on the one hand, the Economy of Communion requires "new people" who are capable of putting into practice the culture of giving in a new society that puts solidarity and sharing at the heart of its understanding of relationships. On the other hand, the Economy of Communion itself, as an economic structure, is a business that spreads "communion." It constitutes a remarkable qualitative leap forward for the future of a better society that is more human, and humanizing, that is more welcoming, and that makes space for men and women to live together in greater dignity.

✧ A Different Economic Dimension: The Experience of the Economy of Communion

Alberto Ferrucci
Prometheus S.p.A., Genova, Italy

I had already come into contact with the spirituality of unity and the Focolare Movement many years before Chiara Lubich launched the Economy of Communion project in 1991. I was working in a company that had constructed a major new oil refinery. Just as it started producing, I was nominated as the Administrative Delegate. I decided to take on this delicate task, making use of the "method of unity." For me, this meant sharing everything about how the business was going with all the personnel, from the directors to the administrative and commercial staff, to the technicians in the refinery. It meant sharing the successes when deals were being signed, the technical innovations that were coming about, and the financial difficulties that arose from lack of investments and under-utilizing plant capacity, as well as the economic uncertainty resulting from the financial system and the political situation.

In this way, through open assemblies that everyone could participate in, I was able to share with all the workers news about the company—news that workers do not normally have access to but is reserved for a small group of business directors.

The resulting widespread awareness of the difficulties that the company was facing, as well as the innovative capacities that had enabled us to face these difficulties, in my opinion, was the winning formula that allowed us to ride the storm that many businesses in our sector were unable to overcome during those years. The unity of intentions and shared commitment among all transformed the industrial complex, which the experts had

31

defined as "the wrong refinery, built at the wrong time in the wrong place," into one of the most productive businesses in the country.

My experience from that time, as well as the experience I have gained subsequently in different contexts, has reinforced my conviction that the success of productive activities depends, to a great extent, on the unity or disunity of those working within them.

Involving all the workers in the business's objectives can create a supportive atmosphere in which people do not feel intimidated nor compelled to take advantage of others, but can fulfill their potential and creativity. It not only adds value to the shares of the company, but also can lead to better quality products and form the basis of future contracts and development. No robot or computer could ever be the substitute for this.

When all those engaged in work—from the workers to the directors—manage to build a "social body directed toward the common good" without losing their individuality, many times they seem to repeat a natural phenomenon in the field of the economy: when the photons of light in a crystal, by means of a technical process, are oriented toward one direction, they turn into a laser that is capable of cutting through steel.

Subsequently, I became an entrepreneur, and when the Economy of Communion project was launched, I saw it as a radical proposal to put the human person right at the center of economic activities.

The Economy of Communion involves entrepreneurs directly as the main protagonists in the market economy. The fact that it starts with entrepreneurs is fundamental, since entrepreneurial style shapes the whole of the business, defining its course of action and priorities. In the Economy of Communion, the entrepreneur is not identified with the stereotypical *homo economicus*, for whom profit is the only goal and *rational egoism* is the only rationale. Luigi Einaudi, a liberal economist and former President of the Italian Republic, challenged this stereotype. He drew attention to the fact that the motivations of business people are actually far more complex. His words are now often found on the walls of the offices of entrepreneurs:

> Millions of people work, produce, and save despite everything we can invent to annoy them, block them and discourage them. It is a natural vocation that motivates them, not just a thirst for money. They relish and take pride in seeing their businesses prosper, in acquiring credit, in inspiring the trust of an ever-growing clientele, in increasing their systems, in decorating their offices . . . all of this constitutes a thrust toward progress that is far stronger than earnings. If this were not the case, then there would be no explanation for all those entrepreneurs who put all their energy and all their capital into their businesses only to take out profits that are modest in comparison with those that could have been made in other ways.

To these motivations, Chiara Lubich adds some others that go even more to the heart of being human, to the "new person" who lives in the depths of each person:

> In contrast to the consumerist economy, which is based on a culture of having, the Economy of Communion is an economy of giving. This could seem difficult, challenging, even heroic, but this is not so, since man, who is made in the image of God, who is love, finds fulfillment in loving, in giving. He experiences this need in the depth of his being, whether believer or not. It is this consideration, backed by our experience, that gives us the hope that the Economy of Communion will be spread universally.[1]

The experience that Chiara Lubich is referring to is the fifty-year history of the Focolare Movement. Right from the start of the Movement in Trent, during the Second World War, Chiara and her first companions felt the need to respond to the love of

---

1. Chiara Lubich, Interview with Polish television, August 1991.

God. They discovered God as their Father, and wanted to make the ideal of unity their own, the ideal of a united world that was proposed by Jesus at the Last Supper when he said: "Father, may they all be one" (cf. Jn 17:21).

During the war, they decided to do this by putting those most in need at the top of their priorities. They sought them out one by one in the most run-down areas and cared for them. They also offered them a place at their table, in their own home, giving them the place of honor and the best tablecloth, since they knew God chose them.

Many people from Trent at that time became caught up in the lifestyle of Chiara and her first companions, and in a few months, amidst the bombs, there was a community of five hundred people who shared their lifestyle. In that community, the miracle of the first Christian community was repeated: "There was no one in need" (cf Acts 2:45). The main hallway of the house where Chiara and her companions lived was always full of sacks of flour, potatoes, clothes, and shoes, which people brought. These were distributed and immediately more things took their place.

Since then, the Focolare Movement has continued this practice of sharing what is extra in order to help the poor and to share the cost of spreading the Movement throughout the whole world. In the 1960s, a center of study, work, and witness to this life of unity was set up near Florence. In time, this has been transformed into a real little town with productive activities. There are now twenty-three of these towns throughout world.

In 1991, Chiara passed through the city of Sao Paolo on her way to the little town of Araceli. She was struck by the fact that alongside one of the highest concentrations of skyscrapers in the world, there is an endless expanse of *favelas,* ramshackle dwellings, in which there were also people who lived her ideal of unity. At that moment, she felt the urgency to provide for their basic needs—food, shelter, healthcare, and, where possible, work—at least for those Brazilians who were close to her, for whom the communion of goods of the Movement had not been sufficient.

When she reached Araceli, certain of the generosity of the Brazilians, Chiara launched the idea of the "Economy of

Communion in Freedom." It was an invitation to the two hundred thousand members of the Movement in Brazil to freely work together—"we are poor, but we are many"—and to initiate profitable productive activities near the little town that would be able to create jobs. These activities would be entrusted to well-qualified people.

What is so "new" about this project? The idea Chiara was proposing was a kind of "productive communion," which would supplement the sharing of surplus already taking place. Alongside the existing small-scale productive activities of the little town, which were used to support the formation schools, she envisaged the creation of a proper "industrial sector," turning the little towns into "pilot towns" where the "culture of giving" would also be put into practice in economic activities. The businesses, moreover, would also create work in different sectors and share their profits.

Chiara, therefore, was not only suggesting that we business people produce useful and high quality products with professionalism and creativity, but that we also run our businesses transparently, paying taxes and not bribes, without polluting or engaging in unfair competition. She was proposing, moreover, that the profits created in this way should be used not only to increase the size of the businesses, but shared—freely—to help our closest brothers and sisters in need and to spread the culture of giving. All this should be done without forgetting to leave space within these concrete economic actions for God's intervention (for those who believe)—drawn down by the constant search for unity.

In other words, it is a vision of the economy based not on the struggle to dominate, but rather on a "commitment to grow together," risking economic resources, creativity and talents, to share profits with those who tend to be excluded from the current economic system because they are "unproductive."

It is a proposal that, at first glance, may seem difficult to accept, but it is also extremely topical and profoundly relevant. Economic well-being, in fact—obtained at the expense of the excluded—does not produce happiness or peace, not even for those who seem insensitive to the suffering of others. Evidence of this is the mounting cost of defending oneself from the desperation of the least through security fences and enclosed neighborhoods.

On the other hand, everyone has experienced the fullness and joy that comes from giving and from providing freely for the needs of family members who are not in a position to help themselves. The Economy of Communion proposes opening up the horizon of this natural family to the "family of unity"—which is already "one heart and one soul"—and then to the whole human family, so that it may become one.

It is natural for entrepreneurs to see their businesses as projections of themselves through which they can accumulate the resources produced. They invest everything in the businesses only to discover at the end of their lives that their children, on whom they were counting to continue the businesses, either do not have the talent to do so or that they would rather "become poets." The "culture of giving" proposes sharing the fruits of their efforts during their lifetimes rather than allowing them to accumulate, perhaps, with the intention of starting a foundation, hospital, or an art gallery, guaranteeing their place in history through marble busts which they will not even have the satisfaction of seeing.

In the past eight years, more than an economic fact (in financial terms it is still of negligible proportions), the Economy of Communion in Freedom has represented a *commitment* on the part of those who have chosen the culture of giving, to demonstrate that it is possible—within the market economy environment—to put into practice an alternative kind of economic action.

It is a transparent kind of economic action that, in an economy that likes to believe that "business is business and nothing else should interfere," often represents the "narrow door." It is a door that the Economy of Communion businesses manage to pass through primarily because of the unity that exists between the business managers and the workers, and thanks to the presence of creativity, which believers would say is one of the gifts of the Holy Spirit drawn down by unity.

The Economy of Communion has been an even more radical choice for those young people (and less young) who wanted to show their commitment to the project and improvised as entrepreneurs, and who now are paying the price of their inexperience. It has also been a choice for those academics who, in order to study the first Economy of Communion businesses close up and to prepare theses on the topic, have endured long journeys around the world. Forty theses on the topic have already been defended, and there are over a hundred currently being prepared.

Various universities across Europe, Latin America, Asia and Australia are organizing seminars and congresses to examine the evolution of this new experience. Recent ones also took place in the little towns of the movement at Hyde Park, New York, in the USA and at Araceli in Sao Paolo, Brazil. Other conferences have been hosted by the University of Santiago del Chile, the University of Antioquia in Medillin, Colombia, the University of Caracas, Venezuela, the little town of O'Higgins in Argentina, the little town of Pace in the Philippines, and at the Catholic University of Piacenza, Italy. The Bocconi University in Milan, Italy, has recently started a permanent observatory on the project.

Around 761 businesses are currently participating in the project. They are all small and medium-sized businesses, which implies a high degree of vivacity. At Sestri Levanti, a small town in the Liguria region of Italy, a business that started with three artisans has now been transformed into a complex that employs 420 people. In some parts of the world the businesses have linked up. In Germany, for example, a group of entrepreneurs set up *Solidar Capital*, a holding company dedicated to the development of Economy of Communion businesses in Eastern Europe and the Third World. It is currently promoting the development of businesses in South Eastern Europe and the Middle East.

There are industrial park projects near the Movement's little towns in Brazil, Argentina, and the United States. There are currently five businesses in the Brazilian industrial park: a clothing factory, a plastics manufacturer, a cleaning products company, a distributor of medicines and sports food supplements, and a finance company at the service of the Economy of Communion businesses in Brazil. This industrial park is administered by a company with three thousand share-holders, many of whom are small investors who live in shanty-towns who raised the five dollars necessary to participate by setting up small cottage industries.

More than three hundred businesses shared their profits in 1998. These profits were used (together with a special contribu-tion from the members of the Movement, since the profits from the businesses are not yet sufficient) to help seven thousand people whom the Movement was unable to help previously. In this way, the experience of the first community in Trent, in which the communion of goods meant that no one was in need, has been repeated on a global scale. Those in need form an inte-gral part of the project. At this time they are only able to "give" their need, but they are always ready to help those who are worse off. Yearly many families who have already been helped make it known that they are able to do without future assistance so that others can benefit from it.

Can this project spread and help humanity, scarred by atroci-ties and the destruction of nature, in its search for peace? The project is certainly not proposing a new economic model *but a new economy for new people who live the culture of giving*.

It is difficult to deny the urgent need for a new culture that transcends consumerism, whether in politics, the economy, or in finance. The Kyoto Environment Conference, for example, demonstrated clearly that the current strain of globalization —based substantially on consumer values—is unsustainable. Such an economy cannot be applied to the whole planet for the simple fact that the resulting climatic change would not allow for it.

The need for this new culture is also demonstrated by the fact that the most industrialized countries in the North—the main protagonists of this development model—today consume fifty-two percent of the renewable oxygen in the earth's atmo-sphere, while representing only sixteen percent of its population.

We believe that a different kind of development, which is attentive to social justice and the environment, in which the gulf between the rich and poor no longer continues to deepen, can be reached only if a new culture, the *culture of giving,* spreads. This culture makes it possible for people to face the difficult challenges of the future without feeling alone.

A Filipino entrepreneur who left her job in a bank and started a consultancy business for the Economy of Communion, explained why this business had become an important player in their sector in South East Asia: "God helps us because we have many brothers and sisters to provide for, and children who, if not helped, will go blind."

It marks a return to the truest human values capable of directing economic action and a new determination to follow one's conscience, expressed in a new, higher, rationality, exalted by unity between workers and managers, with suppliers and clients, with the public authorities and, above all, those excluded from productive economic activities.

This gives rise to businesses in which everyone—even if he or she does not work or invest in them—feels he or she has a stake. These businesses create work and the shareholders share their profits to help the poor and to spread a new culture. They are therefore "living" examples of the social function of the business, which is stressed so much by Christian social doctrine: the capitalist becomes a precious brother or sister who risks what is his or hers for the advantage of all.

In a business like this—and between such businesses—a "capital of relationships" is formed, which cannot be measured in millions of dollars. It is a kind of capital that no one can take possession of through financial maneuvers or speculation. It is capital that will help to overcome difficult times. Such capital will not be created in businesses where the management is convinced that it is worth increasing productivity through exacerbating personal rivalries. Such a belief—that economic success is obtained through reaching the greatest discord between people—leads people toward a "rational" egoism that feeds on their worst instincts.

On the other hand, the capital of relationships is created in an environment of trust, where everyone is free to give in accordance with his or her duties. The success of your colleague becomes your own; whoever wishes can apply innovations. Through emulating the one who does best, the hope of improvement will grow. It will give rise to economic development, which is based on "reciprocity," on giving without expecting a return and the joy of an unexpected return. It is something which is not always easy to reach, but is not impossible for "new people." Those who are believers know that Jesus promised to those who try to live like this that since he will always be at their side with his peace and his providence, he will also be there in their economic results.

These can sometimes take the form of unexpected profits, but they are often the result of ingenious and innovative technical solutions or successful new product ideas. Such things emerge, almost by magic in this atmosphere of peace and bear the mark not only of personal fulfillment, but also the fulfillment of the whole working group.

✧ Toward an Economic Rationality "Capable of Communion"[1]

Luigino Bruni
University of Padova, Italy

The specific behavior that has come into being with the experience of the Economy of Communion and in other similar realities with strong relational and ideal content can be understood only by rethinking and enriching the idea of rationality as it is used today in the science of economics. This is the thesis on which this paper is based. In it, there is an attempt to critically review the current idea of "rational action" in the economy, analyzing its two main points: *instrumentality* and *individualism*.

After briefly outlining the historical-methodological process that led to the current definition of rationality (No. 1–2) and describing its principal characteristics (No. 3), this paper focuses on two recent attempts to enrich the concept of rationality which, in some way, move beyond individualism and the instrumental vision: "Game theory" (No. 4) and "the we-rationality" (No. 5). It seeks to show that the "we-rationality," in particular, when compared with the conventional understanding of rational behavior, offers new significant insights that are close to the vision that emerges in the spirituality of unity. In the final sections (No. 6–7) there is an attempt to begin to outline some

1. I would like to thank Benedetto Gui with whom I discussed many of the theoretical passages of this paper and its current layout in this book. I would also like to thank Vera Araújo, Jesús Castellano Cervera, Piero Coda, Luca Crivelli, Alberto Ferrucci, Gérard Rossé, Alba Sgariglia, Stefano Zamagni, Giuseppe Maria Zanghí, and the participants of the seminar "Reflections on the Economy of Sharing" held in Hamburg, 11–13 September 1999, for reading and critically commenting on the first draft of this paper.

elements of an economic rationality which I have called "rationality capable of communion," seeking to show their relevance and originality.

1.   Introduction

The affirmation of the value of the individual person, of his or her uniqueness and rights, is certainly one of the great inheritances of the West, and in particular, of Christianity.

In other cultures, in general, the point of reference was the clan, the tribe. The "subject" was lost in the community like a drop in the ocean, in which the drop only had meaning if it contributed, with the other drops, to creating the sea: but once it reached the sea, there was no more trace of the drop, of its individuality. In this way, the value of the individual was entirely linked to that of the community; it did not exist before and outside it.

With the Judeo-Christian revelation, the individual acquired a dignity and very high value, and "became" a person. Likewise, history and terrestrial realities also took on an enormous value and were no longer regarded as shadows of a true reality that was transcendent. In the modern (Western) world, technology and science cannot be understood without this process of the valorization of the human person.[2]

The date normally cited as the beginning of this valorization is that of the time of humanism:[3] but, strictly speaking, the beginning of this process dates back to the stable in Bethlehem.[4] The whole of the medieval period, and the synthesis of Christian thought which was carried out by the Fathers of the Eastern and

---

2. One recent authoritative study on this theme is Emanuele Severino, *Crisi della tradizione occidentale* (Milan, Italy: Marinotti, 1999).

3. Cf. Eugenio Garin, *L'umanesimo italiano*, (1947; reprint, Bari, Italy: Laterza, 1994).

4. Within the Greek world one can already see a certain valorization of the individual and his dignity (one only has to think of the democracy that was typical of that culture), which had given rise to philosophical categories that largely informed the definition of a Christian concept of the person.

Western Church even earlier, can also be regarded as part of a process of becoming increasingly aware of the dignity of the person, and of the formulation of adequate philosophical and theological concepts to express this.

All of the modern sciences, from philosophy to politics, from physics to the more recent social sciences, came about through the vindication of their autonomy, in the name of the value and dignity of the human person, as well as his or her works and knowledge. It is not by chance, therefore, that the sciences and technology, understood as the domination and separation of different realities (so as to dominate them), are a peculiar product of the West, and therefore, in a certain way, of Christian culture. Severino, who has been reflecting for decades on the foundations of science and technology, writes: "Scientific specialization, in general, involves the separation of a certain ambit which is considered to be sufficiently autonomous, so that it can be analyzed. A species is that which is visible; and it is visible in the measure in which it is separate, different from whatever surrounds it."[5]

Economic science is one of the places where the affirmation of the value of the individual-person has found its greatest expression. The work of Max Weber, who linked the birth of capitalism to Christian culture (Calvinist in particular), is well known. More recently, there have been studies that specifically cite the valorization of terrestrial realities and human work as the humus in which modern capitalism could develop (the roots of which can be found in medieval times).[6]

Economic science came about as a reflection autonomous from the "moral" dimension, where the action of the individual (intent on maximizing his or her personal wealth) was picked out as the specific point on which to focus. From an indistinct study of human affairs, the economists of the second half of the

---

5. Severino, *Crisi della tradizione occidentale,* 112.
6. Cf. Max Weber, *The Protestant Ethic and the Spirit of Capitalism,* 3d ed. (Los Angeles: Roxbury Pub. Co., 1991). Also see Michael Novak, "The Catholic Whig Revisited," *First Things* (March 1990): 39–42; Robert Sirico, "The Economics of the Late Scholastics," *Markets and Morality* (February 1998): 122–129.

eighteenth century began to pick out their "slice" and to focus on that.

The premise that set in motion Western science, and also economic science, was this: there are no inseparable bonds linking the various aspects of reality.

But economists did not only distinguish and separate out the sphere of "search for wealth" from the others; they also brought about another separation, which I will focus on in this paper. Economics starts from the premise that individuals are not linked to each other by inseparable bonds before beginning to barter. The intellectual exercise of separating the *ego* from the *alter* is, therefore, possible, giving rise to an individualistic science in which "I," as the individual agent, can be analyzed independently of my relationship with the other.

2. From the Value of the Individual to Individualism

Naturally, the affirmation of the individualistic approach was a gradual process that took up more than a century.

The first economists, in fact, were much less individualistic than those today. It was not so much a question of virtue, but the simple fact that, in its early stages, economic science was not very easy to distinguish from the other spheres and not very "distinctive." Economists in the eighteenth century and the first half of the nineteenth century were concerned with everything that had to do with wealth: from work to population, from ethics to psychology, from the class struggle to public happiness.[7] Their era was one of a kind of "social" analysis, since it could not be any other way.

The methodological caesura came at the end of the nineteenth century when, thanks also to the dawn of mathematical analysis

---

7. Nowadays in economics there is a return to this comprehensive approach. This current return, however, can only be compared with that in the early stages of economic reflection on a superficial level. Even when economists stray into other disciplines (which is happening more and more), they are doing it with their instruments and comparing themselves with fields of knowledge that are distinct and autonomous.

and quantitative methods, economists brought about a qualitative leap in the process of separating out their own "slice" of reality. They began to focus their efforts on the action of the solitary and solipsistic *homo economicus* whose aim was to maximize his personal advantage.

From this moment onward, economists have explained every kind of phenomenon, starting with individual behavior, as separate and independent of other phenomena, and use this to interpret and analyze social realities. This approach was called "methodological individualism" at the turn of the twentieth century, and is associated with the Austrian School. It is no coincidence that during this same period, the metaphor of "Robinson Crusoe"[8] became popular in economics manuals. Economics became a science that had no need whatsoever of the native Friday, since Robinson himself also presents an economic problem in the choices he has to make and his individual preferences (for example over whether to work or rest) in order to maximize his objectives.

It was at that point that the value of the individual degenerated into individualism, in the sense that phenomena, which cannot be reduced to the actions of separate individuals, were no longer of interest to conventional economic science.

It is precisely this methodological individualism which many of the critiques launched at economic science over these two centuries, from Marxist to fascist corporativism, have tried to unhinge. In its place they have proposed a holistic approach in which the central focus shifts to classes, society or the state. What all these criticisms share is their denunciation of the inadequacy of using the isolated individual and his actions in order to describe economic and social phenomena.

Such critiques have not, however, prevented the desired effect for the simple reason that the actions, preferences, and choices of the individual are much more real, concrete and able to be

---

8. Further references to this point and more general historical aspects that are only mentioned here can be found in Luigino Bruni, *Economy and the Interpersonal Dimension—A Historical Search of the Roots of its Absence* (Forthcoming, University of Padova, Italy).

analyzed than those of a collectivity, of the state or a vague "we." From here onward the individual took on an absolute status in economics, along with the implicit and often involuntary discrediting and disinterest in everything that cannot be reduced to purely individual choices and preferences.

3.   Individualistic Instrumental Economic Rationality

3.1   Rationalism as an optimal relationship between means and ends

This individualistic formulation of economic science is now enshrined, above all, in the two pillars underpinning the idea of economic rationality: instrumentality and philosophical egoism.

The idea of "economic rationality" plays a key role in economics since it expresses the idea of "optimal behavior" that economists have in mind when they construct models to describe and interpret the world.

This idea, in the way that it is currently present within economics, has distant roots, which can even be traced back to Aristotle[9] and his concept of rational action as the choice of the best means to satisfy personal objectives, an approach which is nowadays called *instrumental*.[10] Reason guides us in satisfying our desires in the best ways, but does not question the content of the desires themselves. This means that behavior will be judged not on the basis of its intrinsic content, but rather on its capacity

---

9. Here I am referring to a tract of Aristotle's *Téchné* and not to the comprehensive vision of action that emerged from his *Nicomachean Ethics* or *Metaphysics*, in which there is a description of human action that is much richer than instrumental logic.

10. "The standard definition of rationality is an instrumental understanding of human action." Hamish Steward, "A Critique of Instrumental Reason in Economics," *Economics and Philosophy* 11 (1995): 57–83. In a citation on page fifty-nine he quotes Nozick as saying: "Instrumental rationality is the common theory, the one which all those concerned with rationality can take for granted." Cf. Robert Nozick, *La natura della rationalità* (Milan: Feltrinelli, 1995), 182. It has also to be added that many great economists (Keynes, Schumpeter, Hayek, and others) had an idea of rationality that was richer and more complex than simple instrumental rationality.

to obtain those results. It is easy to see how such a vision of rationality provided an easy way for *values* and intrinsic motivations of actions to be omitted from economic science. It is the relationship between means and ends and not the content of the ends and means in themselves, which determines the rationality of the action.[11]

The instrumental approach to rationalism is expressed in the idea of *maximization* (of utility). Interpersonal relationships are also normally inserted within this approach to rationality: "Friendships are good or, in other words, useful."[12]

3.2 Philosophical egoism

The other characteristic which is prevalent in economic rationality is what Martin Hollis has called *philosophical egoism,* through which the individualistic formulation of economic science is embodied. One recent publication, for example, says: "One can assume that individuals possess every imaginable set of complicated desires that they try to satisfy through purchasing. The desires can be 'good,' 'bad,' 'egoistic,' 'altruistic'—whatever you like."[13] All that is required is that the objectives should be "individual."

Once these preferences of the subjects are established, the rational criterion is translated into the maximization of the function-objective, in accordance with the rules of formal logic related to individual preferences.

In this vision of rationality, therefore, the ego only enters into an instrumental relationship with alter—when and if it needs to—and interpersonal relationships are thus reduced to a means. Individualism and instrumentality are therefore the two sides of the same coin.

---

11. One author who develops an idea of reason as subordinate to passions is David Hume. Almost one century after Hobbes, he constructed a system in which reason is seen as the "servant" [serva] of passions: *rationality is instrumental* to our objectives. The English scholar, Jeremy Bentham, also followed the same lines.

12. Thomas Hobbes, *De Homine* cited in Roberto Esposito, *Communitas. Origine e destino della comunità* (Turin, Italy: Einaudi, 1998), 12.

13. Shaun Hargreaves Heap, Martin Hollis, and Bruce Lyons, *The Theory of Choice: A Critical Guide* (Cambridge: Blackwell Publishers, 1992).

Despite the fact that the individualism of economic science has survived every kind of criticism and come out strengthened, the number of economists who are dissatisfied with this prevalent definition of economic theory is constantly growing. They have become aware that leaving out the relational dimension of the economy prevents them from understanding many aspects of economic realities and behaviors.

4.   Game Theory and the "Dilemmas" of Rationality

Game Theory has been considered—at least by its founders—as a way to eliminate a certain kind of individualism from economic science. Let us consider whether this is so.

Substantially, Game Theory is a language used to describe economic interactions that are represented as a kind of "game." The roots of the idea are quite old, but mathematicians developed it in the 1920s. They tried to create programs to "rationalize" the strategies of games like chess or poker. With the introduction of Game Theory—which today permeates almost the whole of economic science—economists started to think of economic behavior not only in rational terms (the reason behind which is "which course of action will best satisfy [maximize] my objectives?") but in strategic terms ("which course of action will maximize my objectives taking into account the actions of the others who are taking part?").

Before the introduction of Game Theory, and the idea of strategic rationality, economic action could have been compared to the game of solitaire in which all the cards are hidden.

It is interesting to note that the introduction to the Magna Carta of modern Game Theory[14] refers back to the economy of Robinson Crusoe. It states that in Game Theory Friday has returned to economic science.

Game Theory is certainly a step beyond the "Robinson" individualism that characterized the first synthesis of modern

---

14. John Von Neumann, and Oskar Morgenstern, *Theory of Games and Economic Behavior* (Princeton, NJ: University Press, 1980).

economic science (1850–1940)—since in the games you always start with two.[15]

The extensions of Game Theory "as a rational and logical language for understanding human interactions" are extending far beyond economics, and having a bearing on political science, sociology, psychology, and even military science. In this way, economic rationality is being extended imperialistically beyond its classical boundaries.[16]

One game, which has been particularly useful in highlighting the traps and dilemmas of the individualism contained within individualistic rationality, is the so-called Prisoner's Dilemma. This game is still the best known and well used of the games used within economics and has thousands of variations and complications.[17] A simple analysis of the game shows that it is incorrect to

15. In retracing the forerunners to Game Theory, Morgenstern says this: "Economic theory has to do with two types of variables, which I called 'dead' variables and 'living' variables, the former being those variables which do *not* reflect the decisions made by other economic subjects, while the latter are those which reflect them. . . . Moreover, one needs to specify that even in neo-classical economics there was also a sense of 'two or more'—the analysis of market demand in which the entrepreneur finds himself faced with a number of consumers. But the demand was considered a 'dead' variable like technology, which does not modify the logic behind its choice." Oskar Morgenstern, "The Collaboration between Oskar Morgenstern and John Von Neumann on the Theory of Games," *Journal of Economic Literature* 14 (3) (1976): 813.

16. Cf. Robert J. Aumann and Sergiu Hart, *Handbook of Game Theory with Economic Applicatons,* vols. 1 and 2 (Amsterdam: North-Holland, 1998); Jon Elster, "Marxism, Functionalism and Game Theory: The Case for Methodological Individualism," *Theory and Society* 11(4) (July 1982): 453–82.

17. For those readers unfamiliar with Game Theory it may be useful to summarize the main points of the game. The prisoner's dilemma represents a situation in which there are two prisoners, Luke and Mark, who have been arrested in the enemy camp and have been accused of spying. They are interrogated separately and each of them knows that a) the other is *rational*; b) they have to choose whether to confess or not *without knowing* what choice the other will make (they make their choices simultaneously); c) they have *two* possibilities: to confess ('I am a spy') or not to confess; d) they know that *the consequences* of their choice and that of the other, in terms of the years that they will spend in prison, are as follows: 1) if Luke and Mark both confess, each of them spend two years in prison; 2) if Luke confesses and Mark does not, Luke will be released (due to the rules about confessions) and Mark will spend three years in prison (because he has lied); 3) if Luke does not confess and Mark does, Luke will be imprisoned for three years and Mark will be released (the opposite of the latter); 4) If both do not confess they will only get one year each (there is not enough evidence to accuse them of spying and they are accused of lesser offences). Where does the dilemma

locate the *cause* of the dilemma in egoism: many, in fact, use this "prisoners dilemma" to defend the place of altruism in the economy and to criticize the destructiveness of egoism. Certainly, it does show that with the introduction of a certain degree of altruism some dilemma situations could be avoided. But I personally believe that limiting the problem of rationality, which is hidden behind the dilemma of the prisoner and Game Theory, to the binomial of egoism-altruism is reductive. In fact, if we change the context of the game, we can show that "prisoner's dilemma" kind of situations can arise even when both of the players are perfectly altruistic: but at the same time individualistic![18] As Hollis noted: "It makes no difference whether Adam and Eve (the two players) were headstrong egoists or altruists. The sad result depends only on assuming that Adam and Eve were motivated directly by what each of them, as individuals, wanted."[19]

It is individualism or philosophical egoism—and the instrumental logic it entails, therefore, which is the real cause of the failure of the idea of economic rationality and the edifice of economic theory that has been built around it. This includes Game Theory. In fact, it takes very little to realize that, apart from

---

lie within this simple game? The dilemma emerges if we consider which choices the two players actually make. Let's go back to player number one (Luke). Since he is *rational* he will try to maximize his return *without caring* about the fate of the other. He will therefore reason in the following way: a) if Mark confesses then it would make sense for Luke to also confess (since they will both get two years for confessing; b) if Mark does not confess then it would still be worth his while confessing (he would be released and Mark would get one year). Therefore, *no matter what choice Mark makes it would make sense for Luke to confess*. It is therefore said that in Game Theory *confessing* is the *dominant* strategy for player number one. Since the other player is also *rational*, that is, he will seek to maximize his personal interest, it will also be rational for Mark to confess—it is the dominant strategy also for him. How will the situation end up? What kind of *equilibrium* will result? Both will *confess* and as a result, both will receive two years in prison. Where is the dilemma? It lies in the fact that if both of them had been "less rational" then they would not have confessed (they would have *cooperated*) and only spent one year in prison. *The pursuit of individualistic advantage, in situations where there is interdependence, does not add to the common good or to individual good.* This is the moral of the story.

18. For a theoretical discussion of the dilemmas of altruism see Robert Sugden, "Thinking as a Team," *Social Philosophy and Policy Foundation* 10 (1993): 69–89.

19. Martin Hollis, *Trust within Reason* (Cambridge: Cambridge University Press, 1998), 14.

its declaration of principles and good intentions, the methodology of Game Theory—and therefore a good part of modern economic theory—is still a substantially classical one, and therefore, instrumental and individualistic: "Game Theory offers an elegant and practical logic which can be used to face practical reasoning, giving the most to those who have an idea of rational instrumentality and whose vision of the world is individualistic."[20]

5.   The Second Attempt to Escape from Individualism: The We-Rationality

5.1. A rationality which is instantly sociable

A recent attempt to overcome the individualistic rationality, which seems particularly interesting, is the we-rationality that has been put forward by some authors. Here I am referring in particular to the work of two English authors, Martin Hollis, a philosopher who died recently, and Robert Sugden, an economist, who had been working together for several years to go beyond the individualism in economics. In particular, they suggested moving beyond a rationality of the ego to a we-rationality.

The roots of this idea date back to the work of classical economists such as Smith, Rousseau and Genovesi. The main point is that of developing a concept of rationality in which, in order to decide which action to undertake, a person does not think so much about whether "this action has good consequences for me" as whether "this action is my part in our action, which has good consequences for us."

The cognitive aim of Hollis' operation, which had been developed in close collaboration with Sugden, is that of rethinking the idea of economic rationality in such a way that it can find a sense of sociality while remaining within the realm of reason. His

---

20. Martin Hollis and Robert Sugden, "Rationality in Action," *Mind* 102 (1993): 32. For a demonstration see Shaun Hargreaves Heap and Yanis Varoufakis, *Game Theory—a Critical Introduction* (London: Routledge, 1995), 5–22.

work, in fact, forms the antithesis of those authors[21] who, faced
with the "social damage" created by individualistic and instrumental rationality, are advancing a very different thesis. They
argue that in order to save the social fabric (composed of trust,
morality, reciprocity, etc.), we need to withdraw from rationality
and return to traditional and pre-modern values: "rationality
destroys the very conditions that make human society possible"
is therefore the synthesis of their argument.

Hollis's proposal, on the other hand, operates on a completely
different level. His point is that it is not a question of being in
favor or against rationality, but one of rethinking the very nature
of rationality in such a way that "trust makes sense, given a
different concept of rationality,"[22] which does not destroy
sociality, but strengthens it. "Trust within Reason" is the title of
the book which concisely summarizes his research program.

For Hollis, and others,[23] a notion of sociality has to be inserted
within that of rationality. Hollis holds that through such an
approach it is possible to understand those behaviors that are
relational by nature, but are an anathema to individualistic rationality. He argues that trust and reciprocity "need a more social
concept in order to explain who people are and a vision which is
more linked to their social role, which enables us to understand
why the world goes ahead and helps to express our humanity."[24]
He develops a theory of "rational trust" which is radically

---

21. Fukuyama is one of the best known promoters of this thesis. See, for example,
    Francis Fukuyama, *Trust: The Social Virtues and the Creation of Prosperity* (New York:
    Free Press, 1996). Many of those who are writing about *social capital* are moving in
    the same direction. See, for example, Luigino Bruni and Robert Sugden, "Moral
    Canals: Trust and Social Capital in the Work of Hume, Smith and Genovesi," *Eco-
    nomics and Philosophy* 16 (2000): 21–45.

22. Martin Hollis, *Trust within Reason*, 161.

23. Others who have proposed a "we-rationality" include Susan L. Hurley, *Natural
    Reasons: Personality and Polity* (New York: Oxford University Press, 1992); Marga-
    ret Glibert, *On Social Facts* (London: Routledge Press, 1989); and Robert Sugden,
    "Thinking as a Team." There is also a kind of we-rationality within the works of
    Amartya Sen, *Ethics and Economics* (London: Blackwell, 1987). Backarach has
    recently become interested in *team thinking*. See, for example, M.O.L. Backarach,
    Incorporating Game Theory into the Theory of Action (New York: Oxford University
    Press, Forthcoming).

24. Martin Hollis, *Trust within Reason*, 104.

different from the way that rationality is conventionally understood within contemporary economics, as a result of the role that
the interpersonal dimension plays in it. For this English philosopher trust is a relationship of reciprocity. His understanding of
reciprocity, moreover, is something much deeper than simply
cooperating in order to satisfy one's self-interest (as Hume, for
example, formulated). For this reason, Hollis wants to write a
theory of rationality that makes it rational to rebuild trust, also
when such a way of behaving goes against one's self-interest. For
Hollis, however, trust is only rational between people who have
an interpersonal relationship based on reciprocity: the rationality of trust, therefore, is somewhat different from the moral
obligation set forth by Kant. The expectation that the practice of
trust will become widespread, and that this practice will have
advantages for all, is a pre-condition for the rationality behind
individual acts of trust.

In order to understand this kind of rationality more fully, I will
give you the fine example of three soccer teams used by Hollis in
his book.[25]

He describes the different kinds of logic used by three teams in
a hypothetical championship.

a) The first team, "the Bombers" (marketers) are at the
bottom of the league. They find themselves in this position
for the simple reason that the "rationality" of the
individual players is that of trying to personally score the
greatest number of goals possible. The result is that no one
passes the ball, and all of them try egoistically to score. The
team management has also invested in this kind of
rationality since they offer a monetary incentive and
promotion for each goal scored. The results are disastrous
and the team has lost all the matches (many times the
defense and even the goal is left undefended since the
defenders are also trying to score).

---

25. Martin Hollis, *Trust within Reason*, 106–110.

b) The second team, the "good ones" (Konigsberg Universal), is halfway down the league table. The rule of these players is altruism and they always pass the ball to their companions. They are better than the Bombers, but, they lose several games since instead of taking up the most favorable positions, the offense prefers to pass the ball. As a result, the ones who shoot are not always the best suited to scoring goals. Moreover, taking the initiative is "ethically" discouraged since the players prefer not to attempt difficult dribbling techniques or headers but to pass the ball as soon as they can.[26]

c) At the head of the league table there is the "Musketry" team, who have made "all for one and one for all" their motto. They have chosen to play only for the team. Their joy comes only from the success of the team. Even the less "visible" team members feel proud and happy, since what matters is the team. Their individuality is only meaningful within the team and their personal objectives are those of the team.

Hollis does not associate his proposal of we-rationality with the rationality of the Musketry team, whom he likens more to "donkeys which are obedient to the orders of the farmer, rather than intelligent individuals who possess values which inform their lives."[27] In fact, Hollis poses the following rhetorical question: "At the end of the day, is it possible to be an individual who puts the group in the first place? It sounds like a contradiction in terms."[28] For this reason his proposal is an attempt to marry together the value of individuality (freedom of action) with sociality: "There are, I believe, two ways of understanding the team and, therefore, actions carried out for the benefit of the

---

26. In Hollis's original description, the second team is more complex since there are some Kantian style imperatives and pre-established norms: it is a complex picture which is not needed to make the point I wish to make here.
27. Martin Hollis, *Trust within Reason*, 109.
28. Martin Hollis, *Trust within Reason*, 110.

team. The first is to think of the team as an entity which transcends its members, as a good which transcends and determines the good of the individual components."[29]

Hollis naturally distances himself from this first interpretation of we-rationality (since such a rationality would not represent anything new compared with the traditional concept as it would substitute individual egoism with group egoism).[30] Instead, he indicates what he sees as the correct understanding of rationality: "The other way is to think of team membership as a constitutive relationship between people who remain distinct."[31]

5.2   Inside or outside instrumental rationality?

Here we come to the thorny issue of whether or not the we-rationality represents the substitution of the ego with the group, the substitution of "individual egoism" with "group egoism" within the same paradigm of "instrumental rationality," or whether it is really something new. In particular, within this paper, we want to consider whether this we-rationality goes beyond instrumentality.

In fact, with the we-rationality we are outside the confines of the philosophical egoism of economic theory (since sociality is incorporated in the same idea of rationality). But are we also outside the instrumental approach?

Hollis does not address this question explicitly, but an analysis of his work would place his proposal of rationality within an instrumental one rather than a non-individualistic one.[32]

The answer is therefore more complex. Sugden, whom I have already quoted, is an author who has tried the most to explore this question. In his work, he highlights the danger that we-rationality could represent a cosmetic operation without denting the central idea of instrumentalism, on which the

29. Martin Hollis, *Trust within Reason,* 110.
30. See Pantaleoni's magisterial analysis of this in Maffeo Pantaleoni, *Erotemi di Economia* Vol. 2 (1927; reprint, Bari, Italy: CEDAM, 1964).
31. Martin Hollis, *Trust within Reason,* 110.
32. As discussed in the previous section.

concept of rationality is constructed. As he says: "It is evident that we are going nowhere if, by 'acting as a team member' we mean 'acting in the best interests of the team.' Adopting this interpretation (of the we-rationality) means treating every individual as a rational agent in the conventional instrumental way and that they simply make the objective of the team their own."[33]

How can this problem be solved? For him the way out is to "think of 'membership' as something similar to the ancient meaning which connected arms and legs as members of the same body. Acting as a team member means acting as a component of the team. It is to act within a concerted plan; doing one's pre-arranged part without asking whether or not, given the actions of the others, your own action is contributing more or less to the goal of the team. . . . It is enough for the team members to know that the plan was designed to reach the objectives of the team and that these objectives will be reached if everyone does his part."[34]

So how does this take us out with instrumental rationality? Sugden responds—referring to the work of Hurley—by making the distinction between what is instrumental and what is not in relation to cause and effect: a person who values his actions in terms of the good results produced by those actions is guided by instrumental rationality. A person who is motivated by *we-rationality* and not instrumental rationality, on the other hand, "values his actions as part of a whole made up of the actions of all the team members: for that person an action is rational inasmuch as it is part of the actions as a whole, which, taken together, have produced good results."[35]

What Sugden is trying to say, albeit not in an explicit way, is that it is the motivation that determines whether or not the action of those within a team relationship is primarily instrumental. Rather, it can be explained by starting from a different

---

33. Robert Sugden, "Thinking as a Team," 86.
34. Robert Sugden, "Thinking as a Team," 86. It must be noted that the discussion over the membership relationship in Sugden's 1993 work is much more complex on the level of relational dynamics between team members, than that of Hollis.
35. Robert Sugden, "Thinking as a Team," 86.

logic to the one that relates to means/ends. It is a logic which gives meaning to belonging, to the desire to follow social norms, to duty, to love etc. No one can prevent this action from also being read in terms of instrumentality (and perhaps something can also be gained from that behavior), but the fact remains that the action is not grasped in its specificity nor its peculiarity if only read in this way.

A final consideration

A theory that incorporates the we-rationality can manage to explain phenomena that have remained mysterious within an individualistic paradigm of action. One example is the blood donor relationship.

In 1970, Titmuss, a sociologist from the London School of Economics, published a study of blood donations[36] and reached surprising conclusions that gave rise to a lively debate among economists. One of the most interesting results that Titmuss reached in his field investigation regarded the answer that donors gave to the question "why do you give blood?" In fact, they normally answered: "Because one day I myself or one of my family may need it too." Such an answer makes no sense within an individualistic and instrumental rationality. In fact, the blood that I give today will not be given back to me, nor will the fact that I give blood, mean that I will move quicker up the waiting list when I myself or my family are in need. If all of the subjects were to follow a logic inspired by "economic" rationality, we would find ourselves in a typical "prisoner's dilemma" situation in which no one would contribute. Thankfully, however, people reason differently and continue to give blood. If we were to apply a we-rationality in order to explain this phenomenon we would have to say: "I give blood because I am interested in *our* blood," where "our" signifies my community or also my nation.

There is a difference, however, between my brother and a completely anonymous person. There are also different kinds of

---

36. Richard Titmuss et al., *The Gift Relationship: From Human Blood to Social Policy* (New York: The New Press, 1997).

strangers. Even if I do not know all the inhabitants of my city personally, I feel that they are closer, nearer than those who live in a foreign city, and similarly for my country. The blood donation system works on the basis of this "sense of belonging" to networks of relationships, which are very deep-seated in our psyche. As Hollis says: "For people who flourish within *networks* of relationships, generalized reciprocity is a rational expression of who they are and to what they belong."[37]

It is rational for a we-rationality but irrational for conventional economic rationality.

But how do we explain an attitude of trust, of reciprocity, of altruism, of openness toward the stranger with whom we have no ties or with whom the ties are very tenuous?

Here, Hollis borrows an evocative expression used by J. J. Rousseau, who linked the passage from the private individual to the citizen to a "radical change in man." But he does not explain what this "radical change" consists in, justifying this lack in a phrase that forms the conclusion of his book: "aggressive arrogance toward the questions has to be accompanied by justified humility in the answers."[38]

*   *   *

In the next two paragraphs we will attempt, in the light of the analysis which has been made so far, to draw out some elements of a possible theory of rationality which is better able to understand and explain the dynamics which are being lived within the Economy of Communion. In this experience we can identify the following characteristics:

a) There is a strong sense of belonging to a community, a sense of we that aspires to universal openness;

37. Martin Hollis, *Trust within Reason*, 147.
38. Martin Hollis, *Trust within Reason*, 163.

b) The relationship with the other—which cannot be explained merely in terms of an altruistic attitude—takes on a central value;

c) "Ideal motivations," which are intrinsic and primarily non-instrumental, play a pivotal role;

d) Reciprocity is not linked to the response of the other as a pre-condition, but, at the same time, cannot do without the other's response.

What follows is not intended as a proposal of an alternative to economic rationality in the well-argued and complete sense, but rather an attempt to offer some starting-points for reflections that have yet to be developed.

6.   A Complication in the We-Rationality

The we-rationality undoubtedly offers aspects that are close to the sensitivities of those who are living the experience of "communion" also in the economic field. It enables us, in fact, to grasp many non-individualistic behaviors and, therefore, offers the potential to bring about a rethinking of what rational action is.

At this point, at the conclusion of what has been said up till now, I am anxious to outline some characteristics that, in my opinion, are present in the idea of rationality that emerged from the spirituality of unity, and which can offer a methodological framework to describe and understand better the experience of the Economy of Communion.

If we observe the behaviors that can be found within it[39] and trace them back to the idea of rationality, which motivates them,

---

39. It is worth underlining that the fact that we are emphasizing the experience of the Economy of Communion, which is the topic of this special volume, does not mean that the analysis made is *only* valid for that reality: there are many economic experiences, in particular those with "ideal motivations," which are very close to what is being described.

what could be termed a *rationality of communion,* we can find at least four characteristics:[40]

A. *Universalism.* Above all, the rationality of communion overcomes the group logic between "us" and "them." In fact, if a we-rationality is not matched by openness to universality, it could also be used to describe mafia logic. In the action that creates communion, being part of a particular community goes hand in hand with openness to "universal brotherhood." The "we" of communion opens up to take in the whole of humanity. The "third of the profits" that the Economy of Communion businesses give for the formation of a culture of giving is an expression of this universalism.

B. *Relational dimension.* The person is always seen in a constitutive relationship with the other. One is in a relationship not because he or she has an interest or because he or she is an altruist, but because every decision comes about, *de facto,* from a relationship with someone, from within a relationship. Here, in fact, it is not a case of substituting "me" with "us," but an isolated subject with a subject-in-relationship with the other, the individual with the person. It is an original anthropology, which is different from the one put forward by those who advocate the we-rationality—even if that is the closest thing to it. It is based on the conviction that the person is truly himself only when he gives of himself and welcomes the other, and from this point a new idea of rational behavior is born. The intra- and extra-company relationships that are lived within the Economy of Communion (between business people and their employees, between suppliers and clients, with those who are in need, with the community around the business . . .) cannot be understood outside this

---

40. Clearly the reflections that are presented here are not intended as a schema (even if it is still a work in progress) that can encapsulate the richness of the relationship between the spirituality of unity and the idea of economic action.

relational vision of the human person.[41] But this is more closely linked to the ideas that are developed in the next point, and in the next paragraph.

C. *Expressive rationality.* A rationality that is capable of communion should also transcend the simple instrumental logic. Let's return, for a moment, to the prisoner's dilemma: if the two had decided to cooperate not on the basis of their own instrumental calculations but because they were following ethical norms ("do not betray your companion," or "do not pollute," or "love your neighbor as yourself" . . .) then they would have avoided the inefficient outcome. It is very difficult to locate ethical norms, which are followed regardless of whether it is convenient or not, within an instrumental rationality. They can be likened more to what has recently been described as "expressive" rationality. This term was introduced to indicate economic action that is guided not by a logic that is primarily instrumental, but by the desire to "express" something of one's own personality or one's own values through that kind of economic action. For example, when I bring a bottle of wine to a meal, I don't do it in order to receive something instrumentally, or to meet some personal objective, but because I want to "express" my gratitude to my hosts for their invitation. When I buy an "ethical" product, I don't do so not because I want to optimize my means-ends relationship, but so as to express a value. When I adhere to the Economy of Communion project by putting in common my profits, I don't do so as a result of a means-end calculation, but because I want to express my belief in a certain kind of understanding of the economy and of life. Moreover, if the other sees that there is an element of "instrumentalism" (I behave in such a way as to obtain something in return, or because I hope that the

---

41. Cf. Lubich, "Lezione tenuta in occasione del conferimento della laurea in economia," 7–18.

other will reciprocate) then his "return" lessens and, in certain cases, is reduced to zero.[42]

If Hollis had offered us an idea of expressive (and not instrumental) rationality, in order to explain the rationale behind the soccer teams, we would have to have considered a very different thesis. We would have had to consider that the logic of the team's collective action lay not so much in the different strategies (means) that they put in place to win, but rather in the fact that they enjoyed playing soccer. Expressive rationality, in fact, involves a much deeper level of the dynamic of action. In fact, if we stick with the same analogy, we could say that we play soccer

---

42. The idea of expressive rationality is not a new one. It can be found in the works of Max Weber, who makes the distinction between different kinds of action: instrumental, habitual, affective and "expressive" action, which he describes as "rational in relation to values." This kind of rationality comes into being when the action is motivated "by the conscious awareness of the unconditional intrinsic value of a certain way of acting—whether ethical, religious, or interpretable in some other way—regardless of its consequences." Max Weber, *Economia e Società*, volume 1 (1922; reprint 1961): 22. The English edition of this volume is *Economy and Society: An Outline of Interpretive Sociology* (Berkeley, CA: University of California Press, 1979). Elster takes a similar methodological line: "I would suggest that between the empty theory of rationality and the full theory of the truth and the good there is space for an enlarged theory of what is rational. . . . My suggestion is that we ought to value the wider rationality of beliefs and desires by looking at the way that they are formed." Jon Elster, *Sour Grapes: Studies in the Subversion of Rationality* (Cambridge: Cambridge University Press, 1985), 83. Habermas also says that an "enlarged notion of rationality" with some elements that are "expressive" is desirable. Jurgen Habermas, *The Theory of Communicative Action: Reason and the Rationalization of Society*, vol. 1 (Boston, MA: Beacon Press, 1985). Hirschman adds the point that in general "action that is not instrumental normally makes an individual feel more human. This kind of action can therefore be considered in economic terms as an investment in the identity of the individual and the group." Albert O. Hirschman, *Come complicare l'economia* (Bologna: Il Mulino, 1989), 429. Frey's proposal of "intrinsic motivations" and non-instrumental action is also very close to the concept of "expressive rationality." B. Frey, (1996) "Per cosa, se non per lucro? Lineamenti di una teoria del crowding," *Le organizzazioni senza fini di lucro* (non-profit organizations) (1996). See also David M. Kreps, "The Interaction between Norms and Economic Incentives—Intrinsic Motivations and Extrinsic Incentives," *American Economic Review* (May 1997): 359–364. Robert Nozick also takes the same line with his idea of *symbolic rationality*. Rober Nozick, *The Nature of Rationality* (Princeton, NJ: Princeton University Press, 1994), Chap. 5. It has to be noted that Max Weber developed the idea of rationality within the paradigm of methodological individualism, showing that expressive rationality can be—and usually is—regarded as an individualistic rationality. The aim of this paper is to ask whether there is such a thing as an *expressive we-rationality*.

mainly because we like doing it and then in order to win. If we only consider the second aim, the discussion remains superficial and we are unable to understand why the majority of soccer players play soccer.[43]

7.   Communion and Reciprocity

The fourth characteristic of a rationality of communion is that it is *unconditional* (no strings attached). This enables us to say something about the nature of the relationship between communion and reciprocity, entering into the most intimate and complex part of this research. The specificity of a rationality of communion, in fact, is distinguishable not only by market exchange or by a gift relationship, but by *reciprocity* (with which it is sometimes confused). An element of conditionality is normally associated with our normal understanding of reciprocity: I carry out something; I cooperate so that you will do it too.[44]

---

43. Why—one may ask—can't we also interpret the behaviors that are currently considered as *expressive* in terms of "instrumentalism" (as in the example of the bottle of wine which I take to dinner in order to reach the *aim* of *expressing* my gratitude). Hargreaves-Heap excludes this possibility since from the moment that the action "expresses something of itself" it no longer falls within the framework of instrumental rationality since it undermines the idea of given objectives, which are indispensable in the instrumental approach. The idea of expressive rationality is based on the fact that when an individual acts he or she does not always "calculate" the consequences of his or her action. Moreover, if we read every action as instrumental (from the mother who loves the baby to the martyr who dies for his faith), then besides rendering the idea of instrumental rationality tautological and empty, it does not help us to distinguish between one kind of action and another. In fact, here we are not trying to distinguish between "types of individuals" (expressive or instrumental) but rather to say that the same individuals adopt a different logic in different kinds of actions.

44. Ken Binmore, *Game Theory and Social Contract,* vol. 1: *Playing Fair* (Cambridge, MA and London: MIT Press, 1994 and 1998), 114–115. It has to be noted that some authors, such as Zamagni, Sacco, Crivelli, Kolm, and, in particular, the Austrian School of Fehr and his colleagues, have a richer concept of reciprocity than the one which is normally used within conventional economic theory. Zamagni, for example, writes: "The relationship of reciprocity postulates some kind of balance between what is given and what is received in return, but this balance is not made manifest in the exchange relationship apart from in the relative price. . . . Whereas, in market exchange the determination of the relationship logically precedes the transfer of what is to be exchanged . . . in reciprocal relationships the transfer precedes the object to be exchanged both logically and temporally. The

Even we-rationality contains an idea of conditional rationality.

Is it possible—we must ask—to imagine an unconditional we-rationality, a rationality that is intrinsically social, which does not lay down the response of the other as a pre-condition? This is the same question that Sugden asks at the end of his paper, grasping, in this way, something much deeper in human relationships. His answer is that no, such a rationality does not exist.

Certainly, the instrumentality of the we-rationality is not that of Hume (I will help you as long as you will help me in return). Rather, it expresses the following logic: I will help you because you are my friend, my "partner," and since we are friends we can be considered as a plural agent. In order to be friends, however, a certain kind of reciprocity is required: you also have to be my friend and you have to prove this to me with a certain kind of reciprocating behavior. It is only in this way that we are aware of belonging to the same group, of being a team. This is as far as the idea of we-rationality can take us.

Do the relationships that come about within an experience of communion take us beyond this idea of conditionality?

Yes and no! Certainly there is an element of *gratuity*: the response of the other is not a precondition for my behavior, though it is hoped for, expected or inspired by example.

Does that mean that within a rationality of communion the response of the other is not required? Not at all! This is when the dimension of *time* comes into play. The dynamic of reciprocity, or rather, communion cannot be understood within a static perspective.[45] Even if a rationality of communion is not animated

only fixed point for one who initiates a relationship of reciprocity is the expectation of reciprocity." Stefano Zamagni, *Non-profit come economia civile* (Bologna: Il Mulino, 1998), 39–40.

45. Coleman, the author most widely associated with the idea of *social capital* uses the term *time lag* since it is primarily a sequence of games in which significant phenomena of trust can be verified. James S. Coleman, *Foundation of Social Theory* (Boston, MA: Harvard University Press), 98–99.

by an *ex-ante conditional* rationale, a certain degree of *ex-post conditional* rationale will exist.[46]

Openness to the other has a certain element of ex-anti gratuity, which is unconditional, but for the relationship to continue over time, for the game of the Economy of Communion to succeed, the other has to take on an attitude of response, of reciprocity.

This initial gratuity, however, has a great value in human relationships, also in economic ones. Recent experiments in economic theory[47] show that in interactions (or games) based on trust, the subject has the incentive to reciprocate trust if he knows he has first received unconditional trust from the other. The feeling that we are worthy of trust, therefore, changes us and makes us more capable of reciprocity. Receiving trust from the others, at the end of the day, makes us better people. In other

---

46. There is a passage from the gospel, which, in my mind, expresses this idea very well: "And so the kingdom of heaven can be compared to a king who decided to settle his accounts with his servants. When the reckoning began, they brought him a man who owed ten thousand talents; but he had no means of paying, so his master gave orders that he should be sold, together with his wife and children and all his possessions, to meet the debt. At this, the servant threw himself down at his master's feet. 'Give me time,' he said 'and I will pay the whole sum.' And the servant's master felt so sorry for him that he let him go and cancelled the debt. Now as this servant went out, he happened to meet a fellow servant who owed him one hundred denarii's; and he seized him by the throat and began to throttle him. 'Pay what you owe me' he said. His fellow servant fell at his feet and implored him, saying, 'Give me time and I will pay you.' But the other would not agree; on the contrary, he had him thrown into prison till he should pay the debt. His fellow servants were deeply distressed when they saw what had happened, and they went to their master and reported the whole affair to him. Then the master sent for him. 'You wicked servant,' he said 'I cancelled all that debt of yours when you appealed to me. Were you not bound, then, to have pity on your fellow servant just as I had pity on you?' And in his anger the master handed him over to the torturers till he should pay all the debt." (Mt. 18, 23–34). The king cancelled the debt without putting any conditions on the servant: there is therefore an ex-ante unconditionality. At the same time, the realization that the servant has not pardoned the debt of his fellow servant, which refers back to a logic of reciprocity—which is noted not by the king, but by a third party which is external to the relationship—makes the king withdraw his trust and break the relationship. This example was suggested to me by Luca Crivelli from the Universitá della Svizzera italiana, whom I thank.
47. A recent review of this theme has been undertaken by Vittorio Pelligra, *The Disclosure of Trust: A Game-Theoretical Approach* (Norwich, England: University of East Anglia, forthcoming).

words, these experiments show that there is a dynamic relationship between ex-ante conditional rationality and the ex-post
response: if I receive unconditional trust, the probability of reciprocating it is much higher.[48]

Conclusions

Is it necessary, therefore, to reject individualistic, instrumental economic rationality? Are we saying that economic rationality, as it is commonly understood, does not explain anything
or, on a normative level, should be discouraged? Not at all! There
are ambits in which that type of rationality can explain something (for example, the working of the stock market or the many
small choices which we make every day which are sustained by
the instrumental logic of "optimizing"), and in cases in which
there is no need to complicate and enrich behaviors with
relationality and gratuity.

On the other hand, in areas where the relationship is complex
and qualitative—and these areas are expanding rapidly within
modern society—it is extremely important to enrich and
complete the current idea of economic action.

It is a well-known fact that consumers are becoming ever
more complicated and, in some cases, more mature. For several
decades now, in the West, there has been a notable development
in experiences of "ethical" or "critical" consumption and saving.
This means that citizens are waking up to the urgency of aligning
their economic choices with their concept of life. Consumers and
savers are increasingly interested not only in "what" they are
buying, but also in "how" the product reached their bakery, and
hence, in its intrinsic value. Ethical investment, the development
of ecological consumption, the Economy of Communion and
other experiences are testimony to this. Many consumer choices

---

48. The experimental results of the Austrian school are very interesting in this
respect. For a review of this literature and its applications for the Economy of
Communion see Luca Crivelli, *Reciprocal Behavior in Economic Theory and Its Implications for the Understanding of the Economy of Sharing. A Survey of Recent Literature*
(Lugano, Switzerland: University of Lugano, forthcoming).

are increasingly "expressive" (I purchase a designer dress, a certain label of trainers, a book . . . in order to express something of me). Can these kinds of behaviors be explained through a conventional instrumental and individualistic rationality? I don't think so. This rationality can only explain marginal aspects of this behavior but *not its substance.* And this is not something which concerns only economists, but has implications beyond economic science. Criticizing the dominant idea of economic action, of rationality, is primarily a cultural activity. It means throwing out the idea that only certain kinds of actions are rational.

In this paper, I hope I have shown that by enriching the idea of rational action, experiences like the Economy of Communion can be regarded not as "irrational" but animated by a different idea of rationality, which is equally valid and, perhaps, more effective.

✧ Sustainable Development and Management: Elements of a New Management Paradigm

Hans Burckart
University of Antiochia, Medillin, Colombia

Premise

In this paper, we will make a relatively long journey. We will start from the concept of sustainable development, which aims to be a global answer to many problems: those of socio-economic inequality, as the source of violence and wars; the problem of the environment, which casts doubt on the future of the human race and which is closely linked to socio-economic problems; and the problem of economic activity, which is currently governed by standards which are unsustainable.

From this paradigm of sustainable development, we will then move on to considering the need for a new hermeneutics of reality, which has to be seen as a complex, interdependent and inter-relational system that is open to the future. Humankind has not yet developed the instruments and capacities needed to face this challenge without falling into a fatal reductionism. The paradigm of sustainable development, therefore, places a new challenge in front of us: *we are in need of a new culture*. At the same time, however, sustainable development leaves open the question of what this new culture must be like.

The second part of the paper puts forward the suggestion that the "Culture of Giving" may represent a valid attempt to respond to the existential question posed by sustainable development. Through starting from a different anthropological standpoint, this culture represents a practical and theoretical social experiment that expresses the paradigm of sustainable development:

an equal society, which is the source of happiness and fulfillment for the human race.

The results form the basis of the specific objective of this paper: to consider the implications that this new culture will have for management. The Economy of Communion, which is the projection of this culture of giving into the socio-economic sphere, offers several lines of enquiry. Through reference to this project and the cultural context in which it emerged, it is possible to delineate five essential steps that are at the bases of sustainable management. These five steps demonstrate that conventional administrative and managerial theory has reached its limits and that many instruments are still lacking in order to reach a new management paradigm.

1. The Signs: Sustainable Development and the Culture of Giving

1.1   Sustainable Development—the need for a new culture

1.1.1 Sustainable Development
and the problem of the environment

It is important to remember that the term "Sustainable Development" was coined in the context of the environment. The dramatic events that occurred at the beginning of the 1970s, like the energy crisis and the prophecies of Meadows,[1] announcing an immanent future of darkness without energy and natural resources, raised people's consciousness of the environmental problem. In this way, the discussion broke out of the closed circles of environmentalists and became a topic that concerned the whole of society, to the point that the United Nations (UN) hosted a conference on these themes in Stockholm in 1972.

From the beginning of this debate, the environment has been a difficult issue. The same polemic has raged between the

---

1. Donella H. Meadows, et al., *The Limits to Growth; A Report for the Club of Rome's Project on the Predicament of Mankind* (London: Pan Books, 1972).

industrialized countries and the developing countries from the Stockholm conference, to the 1997 Kyoto Conference on Climatic Change and the 1998 conference in Buenos Aires, which concluded: "When we have to kick start socioeconomic development, we cannot worry about the environment." In other words, respect for the environmental is regarded as a concept that is the "icing on the cake" for the rich nations.

At the same time, "green" pressure groups started to vigorously attack the traditional concepts of development and the dominant practices in productive sectors, seeing them as the main culprits for the deterioration of the environment. All this has given rise to a lively debate between the ecological activists and the most important economic sectors. It is a debate that is still open.

The term "Sustainable Development," therefore, was coined in a dramatic and highly polemic context.[2] It is not surprising, therefore, that even today this term is still given an exclusively environmental meaning in official documents. Nevertheless, this reductive interpretation cannot comprehend the true dimensions of the idea of sustainable development.

1.1.2 Sustainable development: an integrative concept with a social emphasis

The nineteenth Special Session of the General Assembly of the United Nations (June 1997), which was held five years after the "Earth Summit" in Rio de Janeiro, aimed to evaluate and strengthen efforts to reach sustainable development. The following declarations show how the understanding of the concept has changed:

> The reduction of existing inequalities in the distribution of wealth and access to resources, both within countries and between them, is one of the most urgent problems facing humanity. . . . As a

2. The term was officially used for the first time in a World Wildlife Fund (WWF) document at the beginning of the 1980s in a purely environmental context.

consequence, the eradication of poverty will be one of the original themes of sustainable development in the next few years.[3]

The General Assembly, indicating the practical measures needed in order to reach sustainable development, established three principal tasks for the period 1997–2002. The UN Commission on Sustainable Development decisively underlined the original and universal importance of these tasks for sustainable development:[4]

a. The eradication of poverty.[5]
b. Changes in consumption standards.
c. Changes in production standards.[6]

From this, one can tell immediately that the UN has a concept of sustainable development that goes far beyond a purely environmental understanding. Its main approach, in fact, is a social one and in place of the restrictive environmental vision it has a wider integrative one:

---

3. Nineteenth Special Session of the General Assembly of the United Nations, *Program for the Continuation and Implementation of Agenda 21*, New York, 27 June 1997. See also Rio Conference, *Agenda 21* (1992) chap. 2 and the *Copenhagen Declaration on Social Development,* commitment 2.

4. Commission on Sustainable Development, (CSD) Seventh Session, New York, 19–30 April 1999.

5. The priority actions listed include: 1) Improving access to sustainable income, to entrepreneurial opportunities and to productive resources; 2) Permitting universal access to universal basic social services; 3) The progressive development of social security systems for those who are not economically self-sufficient; 4) Empowering those who live in poverty and their organizations; 5) Pay more attention to the disproportionate effects of poverty on women; 6) Work with interested donors and recipients to direct rises in Gross National Product (GNP) for the eradication of poverty; 7) Intensify international co-operation for the eradication of poverty.

6. Also refer to *Agenda 21*, chap. 2. The UN also uses terms such as "environmental space" and "ecological footprint," as well as concepts which have been developed within specific industrial sectors (eco-efficiency, factor 4 and 10). In general these concepts tend to be reductive in the sense that they do not properly address the social dimension.

We are convinced that in order to reach sustainable development there is a need to integrate its economic, social and environmental components. We re-commit ourselves, therefore, to collaborating—within a spiritual of world solidarity—within the aim of multiplying our joint efforts to meet the needs of present and future generations fairly.[7]

At this point we have reached the key to the idea of sustainable development. It is worth explaining it in some detail.

1.1.3 Principal characteristics and dynamism of sustainable development

The UN World Commission for Environment and Development, the so-called "Bruntland Commission," laid down the basis of the concept of sustainable development.[8]

After four years of work, the commission finally published an exceptional report called *Our Common Future*, which also became known as the *Bruntland Report*. This report became the reference point for all activities relating to the field of sustainable development, and in particular the Earth Summit in Rio in 1992.

The Commission recognized that sustainable development means widening our horizons. It noted that it is not possible to speak about the environmental problem in isolation. It has to be considered as a complex and interdependent phenomenon. Moreover, the report underlined the fact that technology and globalization represent enormous challenges and opportunities for development. All of this gave rise to the need for a holistic, global and systematic vision of our world, of humanity and of the concept of development. Some key elements of this vision have to be underlined:

---

7. Nineteenth Special Session of the General Assembly of the United Nations, cit. No. 3.
8. In December 1983, concerns over the deterioration of the environment led the Secretary-General of the United Nations to call on the then Prime Minister of Norway, Gro Harlem Bruntland, to establish a special independent commission. The aim of this commission was to set out "a global agenda for change."

The Bruntland Commission came up with a definition of sustainable development that is still the same today. "Sustainable development is development which satisfies the needs of the present without compromising the ability of future generations to satisfy their needs."[9] This definition underlines the importance of long-term development, emphasizing future generations.

The idea of "satisfying needs" is clearly central to the commission's vision of development. It affirms, "To make the concept of 'need,' especially the basic needs of the poorest, a clear priority."[10] This definition marks a change: the Bruntland Commission shifts the emphasis in sustainable development from the environmental to the social sphere. From now on it is not possible to associate "sustainability" exclusively, or even primarily, with environmental problems.

Once the commission established the social aspect as a priority, it highlighted the close relationship between the economic, social and environmental aspects: deterioration in one of the aspects will necessarily lead to a deterioration of the others.

After the groundwork of the Bruntland Commission, which was still too theoretical, efforts turned directly to the goal of operationalizing sustainable development. Among the numerous strategies, there are the following:

The Bruntland Commission underlined the importance of creating a comprehensive package of policy measures, which would include economic incentives, internalization of environmental and social costs within market prices, environment and social impact assessments, and regional, national and international information campaigns. Even if the Bruntland Report covered a lot of ground in this respect,

9. World Commission on Environment and Development (WCED), *Our Common Future* (Oxford, England: Oxford University Press, 1991), 43.

10. WCED, *Our Common Future,* 43.

we are still at the beginning of that radical change which all this would entail.

The concept of sustainable development involves a vast theoretical and pragmatic reflection. In particular, new systems of indicators of development and sustainability are needed. The challenge consists in building systems that can manage vast amounts of complexity in an integral way without oversimplifying them in an inappropriate way. Very few scientific instruments that have so far been developed by philosophy, logic and mathematics are able to do this.

The Bruntland Report's definition of sustainable development creates a dilemma, which starts with a question: "What should we do to satisfy the needs of the poor in the world?" The most logical answer is: Increase economic growth so as to generate the most wealth that can then be redistributed equally. The Bruntland Report, therefore, asks for economic growth to increase tenfold. This strategy, however, creates a conflict with environmental limits. Commentators suggest that even doubling current levels of economic activity would surpass the carrying capacity of "spaceship earth."[11] It would seem that there is only one way out of this dilemma: changing consumption and production standards. This would imply new technological paradigms,[12] but also new behaviors, a new culture on the part of consumers.

In other words, the concept of sustainable development brings about an enormous change. The social question becomes central, as it requires a new culture that puts particular emphasis on the eradication of poverty on a global scale. This culture would entail

11. Cf. Herman Daly and John Cobb, *For the Common Good: Redirecting the Economy toward Community, the Environment and a Sustainable Future* (Boston, Mass.: Beacon Press, 1994).
12. Here another strategy comes into play—that of "more with less." The idea that more can be produced with less environmental impact through "resource efficiency," "product lifecycle analysis," "ecoefficiency," "cleaner production," "dematerialization" and so on.

a high degree of respect for nature and would be based on new economic, technological and legislative paradigms, including new production and consumption standards. This culture could be one of the greatest challenges of the new century. We have to realize, however, that we are only just beginning to recognize this change and to develop the necessary elements of this culture.

1.2 The "Culture of Giving" and the Focolare Movement

What elements of this culture, which underpins the idea of sustainable development, do we not yet fully understand? A new and unexpected concept—"culture of giving"—is becoming fashionable.[13] The meaning of this term, however, depends entirely on the context in which it is used. In this case, we are talking about the culture of giving as the Focolare Movement promotes it.

This Movement is based on an interesting and new anthropological vision, which is not deducted so much from theoretical reflections as from the attempt to give a spiritual content to the practice of everyday life. The spirituality that has emerged is valid globally, and is implemented and embodied in very different cultures, faiths and social situations. Its anthropology is characterized by overcoming subjectivism (with all its modern forms in the shape of individualism and liberalism) through a communitarian lifestyle. According to the Movement's vision, the community and the individual are clearly distinct but at the same time inseparable and in a harmonious relationship. Neither of the two precedes the other or dominates the other. This gives rise to a model of inter-subjectivity, which, perhaps, overcomes the few attempts that have been made in the past to tackle this argument.

At this point, what interests us is to see whether the culture of giving of the Focolare Movement offers some elements that could

---

13. Here we can refer to a wide range of contributions starting with Erich Fromm (to have or to be) right to Bill Gates, the founder of Microsoft, who said: "I believe strongly in the link between business and the art of giving." (Cited in an interview with SEMANA, 12–19 April 1999, 884, Bogota, Colombia.)

contribute toward the construction of the "new culture" required by sustainable development. Several interesting points emerge.

The foundation of the culture of giving could be termed as "an interdisciplinary paradigm of unity." The spirituality and praxis of the Focolare Movement constitutes a living example of how to achieve this paradigm in the context of interpersonal and social relationships. This paradigm, however, also constitutes the methodological bases for the construction of theoretical models, strategies, empirical research and application schemes. In other words, the "paradigm of unity" consists in bringing together complex systems to a state of support and equilibrium and a state of "unity" of the systems themselves. This paradigm of unity, therefore, could prove to be vital in reaching sustainable development in all its complexity.

The culture of giving which the Focolare Movement promotes is not an abstract theory. It is part of an internal system of values and attitudes shared by several million people from the most varied cultural backgrounds. It is "tangible" in a particular way in the little model towns, which the Movement calls "citadels."

In the context of the Focolare Movement, the term "to give" does not take on the meaning of "to give a gift" or "make a donation" in the sense which is intended by benevolent, paternalistic or charitable humanism. The term "to give" is understood, rather, as the antithesis of the dominant culture that is based on "having," on "possessing." While the idea of "making a donation" simply entrenches the culture of having (by setting itself out as an exception), for the Focolare, "giving" is at the heart of all the values and most fundamental social dynamics. It is a radical paradigmatic change that involves every aspect of life and creates an enormous potential for the construction of what has been called "social capital,"[14] which is at the basis of development.

The "social space" which is suited to the culture of giving is the "community," understood in the widest sense of the word. Any community or organization or people could be considered as a viable social space in which the culture of giving could flourish.

---

14. There is vast literature on this theme starting with the work of Putnam, Coleman and others.

This coincides with the observations of modern social analysts who describe today's society as a "society of organizations."[15] Moreover, the culture of giving, in the sense that the Focolare is proposing it, can be put into practice between organizations and in this way form a way of relating to each other. It is easy to reach the conclusion that, with a few more steps, the whole of society could acquire these characteristics.

1.3 The culture of giving and sustainable development: the same utopia

It would appear that the Focolare Movement's culture of giving and sustainable development each, in their own way, represent a new effort to fulfill an ancient dream of humanity. It is, perhaps, the most ambitious dream of humanity: to live in a just society where there are no poor. As far as we can tell, human beings have always been aware, to a greater or lesser degree, that this would be the best place in which the ancient problems of violence and slavery could be eradicated; where values and processes that are at the basis of happiness, could be generated. History is full of attempts to build this kind of society. It is enough to think of the ancient civilization of Israel and the first Christian communities (without ignoring the enormous differences between them) and the recent communist and socialist utopias.

The analysis that has been done so far shows that this same dream can be found—whether we are aware of it or not—behind the terms sustainable development and culture of giving. The scheme that follows—without wishing to be exhaustive—illustrates how these two concepts are complementary in this common effort.

---

15. Peter Ferdinand Drucker, *Post-Capitalist Society* (New York: Harperbusiness, 1994), 54–75.

Dimension	Sustainable Development	Culture of giving
World vision	Holistic vision Emphasis on interdependence and interrelationship	Interdisciplinary paradigm of unity
	Emphasis on the logical-systematic dimension Highlighting the urgent need for new scientific instruments	Emphasis on the spiritual-historic dimension The potential for the methodological consolidation of many theoretical models, empirical research strategies and models of application
Understanding of the "time" dimension	Long-term thinking Short-term aspects are deduced from long-term ones	Intense interaction between the present and the future (eschatology or principle of hope)
Objective of the process of development	To satisfy needs (especially the needs of the poorest) Tendency toward reaching a "realistic minimum"	The "fulfillment" of the "human being in community." Happiness Tendency toward "prophetic maximum"
Principal Dynamics	To improve the dynamic interrelationship between the economy, the social fabric and the environment "Win-win" strategies	A new dynamic to guide complexity toward unity Key concept in this dynamic: "giving"
	Emphasis on the prevention and solution of problems	Emphasis on "giving" as a new epistemological principle
Strategies	The construction of a theoretical framework Local, regional and international policies New production and consumption standards	The construction of a theoretical basis (in its initial stages) Living experiences and the construction of "model villages" The Economy of Communion project (with its practical and theoretical dimensions)
	Emphasis still on the environment, but moving toward the social and cultural aspects	Emphasis on social and ontological aspects
Anthropology	Centrality of the human person	Centrality of the "person in relationship"
	Note: Up to this point there has been no reference to an anthropological key Over emphasis on the environment	Note: a new inter-subjective model that corresponds closely to the current vision of a "society of organizations"
A more equitable society without poverty		

2. Economic and Managerial Consequences: The "Economy of Communion" and "Sustainable Management"

2.1   The "Economy of Communion" Project

The Economy of Communion project is the projection of the Focolare Movement's culture of giving into the social and economic spheres. The Economy of Communion contains the elements that were mentioned earlier: it came about as a measure to fight practical situations of poverty and from the start the dynamic of "giving" was central to it. The profits, which are traditionally considered the legitimate property of the owners or shareholders, freely become resources which can be used for clearly defined purposes: for the immediate help of the poor, for rebuilding the long-term social fabric of society (through formation in the culture of giving) and for reinvestment in the business. All of this finds a concrete space in close connection with the so-called model towns, villages that are socially structured according to the culture of giving.

The scope of the Economy of Communion, however, goes far beyond this initial analysis. It also wants to be an attempt to "humanize the economy"[16] and to offer an economic alternative to today's society. The strength of this experience lies in the fact that, while being the projection of the culture of giving within the economic and social sphere, it has all the experience of this "interdisciplinary paradigm of unity" at its disposal.

The Economy of Communion, therefore, stands alongside all those proposals that have taken up the challenge of recognizing the complex, interdependent and interrelational nature of reality that has also been underlined by the concept of sustainable development.

Approaches like the Economy of Communion will no doubt have a macroeconomic value. Nevertheless, the current phase of

---

16. Cf. Chiara Lubich, "Lezione tenuta in occasione del conferimento della laurea in economia," *Nuova Umanitá* 21/1 121 (1999).

the project focuses on the role of the entrepreneur and his relationships both within and outside the business, his identity and
his function in relation to all the intervening factors. In the
current phase of the project, therefore, what is evident is that an
Economy of Communion requires a "business/organizational
culture" of communion or rather, as Chiara Lubich recently
expressed, a proposal of "economic action."[17]

2.2 Administrative implications: "Sustainable Management"

The first outline of a possible new management model can be
discerned if one draws inspiration from the economic projection
of the culture of giving and the complementary approach of
sustainable development. This new model cannot sit alongside
the numerous management models available today, but neither
does it replace them. Rather, it draws out a common thread, at a
more general level, which is often missing in the application of
theories, models and modern instruments.

Having come up with no better terms, we dubbed this model
"Sustainable Management." It can be described in five phases.

Phase 1: What direction are we going?

Management models normally start with the search for the
mission and vision of the organization. It would seem, however,
that even before reaching this stage, it is necessary to ask an even
more basic question: "What is the global context of our busi-
ness/organization?" "What direction is the society that we are
part of going in?" In many cases, ideas, which arise from the
culture of giving and sustainable development, can clarify these
questions and corresponding answers. In this way it is possible to
understand better the context in which the organization or business has to move.

---

17. Cf. Chiara Lubich, "The Experience of the 'Economy of Communion': A Proposal
of Economic Action from the Spirituality of Unity" (Talk given in Strasbourg,
France 31 May 1999). Published in this volume.

Phase 2: Who are we?

It is worth asking what one's (ontological) identity is and what fundamental role the business/organization is playing in relation to the local and global society, in particular in relation to the goal and the "way" which was identified in phase 1. One has to be aware that today's society is a "society of organizations." It is a society, therefore, in which organizations, and not so much individuals or governments, are the principal agents of change. It is only with this self-awareness that one can understand fully the weight of one's organizational or business activity.

Phase 3: What should we do?

This is where the more technical part of the Sustainable Management model begins. Traditionally it was enough to have an initial business idea in order to define the specific role of the business or organization—"we make such and such a product, offer this service, etc. . . ." Within the context of the relational reading of society (which is at the basis of the Economy of Communion and sustainable development), this is no longer enough. We have to ask ourselves what all the interested parties are investing in our business or organization and what they hope to gain from this investment. Traditionally only the shareholders or owners were considered part of this group since they were the ones who had a financial interest and expected a financial return. We also have to consider the workers, who invest their talents, their creativity, their time and their needs and expect their needs to be satisfied, their self-fulfillment etc. One also has to consider the clients, who invest their needs and desires and want them to be satisfied. Then there are also other interested groups who are involved: suppliers, legal authorities, competitors, local and global communities, the environment that "invests" its resources and expects them to be treated in a dignified way. Organizational theory recognizes this approach as a *stakeholder* approach.[18] Many regard this as the basis of future

18. Cf. Peter Vaill, "Visionary Leadership," in Allen Cohen, *The Portable MBA in Management* (New York: John Wiley and Sons, 1993), 12–37.

management. The Economy of Communion proposes the same vision in slightly different terminology.[19]

The key to this shift is the fact that the business/organization is no longer considered the center of interest. Rather, all the groups with which the business has a relationship are the focus. You could say that the business has to "forget itself" in a way, and put itself in the shoes of its stakeholders—all the groups with whom it has a vital link. In this way, the business cannot be regarded as self-determining, but determined from the "outside" by the expectations (visions) of its partners. The sum of the expectations, needs, desires, prejudices and so on, of all the stakeholders defines the vision and the reason for existence of the business. In other words, it defines its mission. This leads to a paradigm shift in managerial culture: the attitude of domination, which is based on the ego, gives way to an attitude of service, which is based on the other.[20]

Phase 4: How do we behave?

Faced with the difficult task of harmonizing multiple expectations, which at times seem incompatible, the question of how to reconcile so many interests arises. Managing to carry out this task is the sensitive business of entrepreneurs and managers today. This is where it is possible to see whether or not one has what it takes to be a leader: whether or not he or she is capable of synthesizing, integrating and transforming all the different visions of the stakeholders into an *operative vision* in which every stakeholder can feel at home and with which each can cooperate

---

19. Chiara Lubich, "Laurea in economia," 7.
20. Clearly this gives rise to a complex model of the organization that is not as easy to manage as the linear models that were used in the past. There are indications, however, that the failure to embrace this kind of vision is the reason behind many recent business failures. See Liz Crosbie, *Strategy for Sustainable Business: Environmental Opportunity and Strategic Choice* (London: McGraw-Hill, 1995). Classical administrative theory uses the method of "limited rationality," which has been borrowed from the natural sciences. It seeks to optimize one parameter (in many cases "profit"), while keeping all other variables stable. This method, which was very successful for a time, now seems inadequate in an era of existential interdependence. Multifunctional mathematical instruments are needed for the systemic model of stakeholders.

effectively. In the first half of the twentieth century, a leader was characterized as a "general"—as one who could take the initiative. Nowadays other qualities are needed. It is not enough to speak, but to listen as well. Commanding is not as important as promoting. One has to be like the conductor of an orchestra who knows which person plays the violin or the French horn best. In other words, he is capable of listening and enabling the talents of the members of the orchestra to emerge, so that from the harmony of all a symphony is born.

Much has yet to be written on the methods of creating this unity that, at times, can seem a difficult task. Here we are going to focus on the need to widen the concepts which permit us to create "unity," and hence equilibrium, in a dynamic and complex system.

Complexity has normally been regarded as the problem. For this reason, the aim has been to reduce it as much as possible, normally through the principle of *exclusivity* embodied in the hierarchy. Nowadays, people are recognizing that it is possible to see things in the opposite way: to see complexity as the solution and to ask what the problem is. In other words, the task is not one of avoiding complexity but "welcoming" it since it is only through it that it is possible to find lasting and new solutions to problems, which are often hidden or confused.[21] It is then possible to reach two *inclusive* principles that create unity. The following table shows some of the uses of these principles.

It is impossible to say which one of these principles is better than the other. There is a correct form that can be used at different times and in different situations. It would be pure fantasy to want to run a multinational company only with consensus. One needs to use models of democracy and, hence, the exclusive idea of hierarchy. Nevertheless, the principles of feedback and support can easily be applied to very large organizations, so long as they are accompanied by a politics of decentralization and *empowerment*. In the case of a team of five or ten people the situation is somewhat different: in general it is highly

21. D. Baeker, "Einfache Komplexität" in Heinrich W. Ahlemeyer and R. Königswieser, eds., *Komplexität managen* (Frankfurt: Gabler, 1998).

unproductive to run this sort of group in a hierarchical style. The circular model is more appropriate, so long as there are not any mitigating circumstances.

	Hierarchy	Circular	Feedback
Unifying principle	Exclusion	Inclusions	Supported inclusion
Process of unification	The exercise of power, domination	Synergy	"Chaos management"[22]
Decision taking	Imposition (dictator) or voting (democracy)	Consensus	Processes
Function	Functions	Processes	Processes
Regulation	Control	Verification	Feedback promoters
Leadership	Power Leadership	Collective Leadership	Service Leadership
Typical structure	Pyramid	Team	Orchestra
Metaphor	Army	Musical Improvisation	Orchestra
Principal attitudes	Speaking, leading, being understood	Speaking, listening, cooperating, understanding	Listening, supporting, speaking, cooperating, understanding, highlighting

Stage 5: Are we on our way?

In following out all these processes, it is possible to forget where you were coming from. It is, therefore, necessary to ask oneself: how do we know which direction we are going in? Are we still in line with the first three stages?

The principles of sustainable development and the culture of giving make us respond to this question by examining our business activity/organization on three fronts: *ecological, economical* and *social*. It is necessary to demonstrate that there is "value added" in each of these three areas. We need to show that *economic* value has been added and according to the stakeholder's

---

22. Cf. Peter Müri, *Chaosmanagement. Eine neue Führungsphilosophie* (Thun, Switzerland: Otto Verlag, 1998).

model. This does not simply mean the maximization of investor's capital. It also entails taking into consideration the satisfaction of the economic needs of the other groups with "economic" interests like the clients, suppliers, competitors and the state.[23]

The establishment of what level of ecological value has been added can be determined through carrying out an eco-balance of the business/organization or through an analysis of the life cycle of the products and services. Many instruments already exist to facilitate this, for example, specialized software packages and reference tools for environmental systems management.[24] Alongside providing a means to evaluate environmental value, these tools can also bring a competitive advantage for the business.

In relation to the third dimension, the social, current administrative theory does not yet have systems that can be used to measure the social value of entrepreneurial activities. In many cases, this dimension is reduced to a kind of ineffective charity, which is at times counterproductive. At the same time, the aim of producing social value has become the goal of non-governmental organizations, which have recently given rise to interesting alliances of groups. In order to evaluate the additional social value it is necessary to move beyond the simple idea of financial support.[25] Alongside the basic subsistence needs of an individual or a family, one has to take into account the other intangible values that are taken for granted at different levels of social organization. This gives rise to a verification system for social value within business, which is summarized in the table on the next page.

---

23. Current management theories in general do not take this complex balance into account and refer simply to the linear model that analyzes the return on investments. There is a need for new models here.

24. ISO 14000 (International Organization for Standardization) at a global level; EMAS (Eco-Management and Audit Scheme) within Europe.

25. Within the context of sustainable development, there are useful systems to measure social development; other approaches make use of concepts such as "social capital," which is put forward by Coleman, Puttman and others.

Level	Tangible variables	Intangible variables
Persons and families	Standard of Living Basic needs Knowledge and ability Occupation and access	Personal Capacities Self-esteem Cultural identity Creativity Critical reflection
Organizations (Non Governmental Oganizations [NGOs], popular organizations, networks etc.)	Managerial Capacity Programming Management Use of resources Sphere of influence and ties	Cultural Organization Vision Techniques for creating "unity" Autonomy Solidarity
Society (local, regional and international)	Local/Civic Space Laws Policies Practices	Social Norms Values Attitudes Relationships

3. Conclusion

It is the task of the next article to demonstrate how management theories such as Continuous Improvement, Strategic Planning, Chaos Management and Value Management can adapt to the challenge of sustainable development and how they can contribute to it. What is often missing from these theories, however, is an underlying thread that links them together. This is the task that this paper has sought to answer.

Two important questions still remain:
a) What is the relationship between management and the new culture that is being proposed? We have discussed business administration, but at the same time, in a more general way, we are talking about administrative organization in general. We have talked about the fact that society today is a society of organizations. Administration, therefore, goes far beyond the realm of the business or an organization. Administration means building a new

culture. The horizons of the business manager today extend far beyond the business, but embrace the whole of humanity.

b) The second question is perhaps surprising: which managers are the protagonists of new cultures? According to the hierarchical model they would have to be the men and women in gray suits that travel business class around the world. We also said, however, that alongside the principle of hierarchy there are two other principles that can be used to manage the complexity of the organizational system. According to these two principles, which are inclusive, all groups or people involved in an organization are "managers"—the employees, clients, suppliers, competitors and surrounding society, and above all the large numbers of poor in the world.[26] It is only together that we can "administer" our society and direct it toward a sustainable future, toward a culture of peace, equality and happiness.

---

26. Chiara Lubich, "Laurea in economia," 7.

✧ Development Problems in Businesses with "Ideal Motivations"

Mario Molteni
Catholic University of Piacenza, Italy

There are some businesses that involve strategic and organizational behavior that cannot be understood without making reference to the ideals that shape their decisions, and to the attitudes of their leaders. The businesses that are part of the "Economy of Communion" project fit into this category.

The critical reflection on this experience contained within this article has two main aims. On the one hand, it emerges from a desire to identify the key aspects of business that have a critical impact on the consolidation and development of the Economy of Communion. On the other hand, there is an attempt to identify what the Economy of Communion can teach us, granted that those who are part of it are motivated by a profound ideal, which they would like to see transformed into a business enterprise within the current social and economic context.

1. An Example of Businesses with "Ideal Motivations"

Businesses "motivated by ideals," precisely as a result of the cultural orientation of their key actors, tend to marry together concern for the needs and demands of a competitive market environment with care and attention to the needs of their workers and to the development of society as a whole. Those in charge of such businesses are committed to demonstrating, through concrete facts, that these two dimensions are not incompatible; and that it is possible to create a synergy effect between them.[1]

On the one hand, in fact, respect for nature and the needs of people unleashes the potential for collaboration at every level, becoming, in this way, an element which promotes the competitiveness of the business. On the other hand, reaching targets in terms of profitability and market position sustains and fosters attention to the human factor. Business success makes more resources available for reaching wider objectives. At the same time, it is tangible proof of the effectiveness of the business project under way: the ideal to which one devotes oneself, therefore, makes an impact on society and creates development, work, quality of life, and spaces for positive human relationships. The awareness of collaborating in this is a source of deep satisfaction for the protagonists.

Through their work, therefore, businesses with ideal motivations find themselves at the heart of the current debate between scholars and practitioners over the compatibility of the logic of maximizing one's personal interest and ethical concerns. Moreover, the experience of many Japanese businesses and many excellent Western ones,[2] as well as the contribution of first-rate economists,[3] have exposed the unreality,[4] and, therefore, the futility, of a framework that makes a structural antagonism between economic objectives and social needs.

Let us move on now to discuss the case of the businesses which are part of the Economy of Communion. Their experiences show, in more or less complete forms, the attempt to give rise to

1. Cf. Vittorio Coda, "Fisiologia e patologia del finalismo d'impresa," *Aggiornamenti Sociali* 2/3 (1988).
2. Thomas J. Peters and Robert H. Waterman, *In Search of Excellence: Lessons from America's Best-Run Companies* (New York: Warner Books, 1988); Gianfranco Rebora, "Le imprese eccellenti: il caso italiano," *Finanza, Marketing e Produzione* (1984).
3. One thinks, for example, of the contribution of Amartya Sen, Nobel economics prizewinner in 1998, who has substituted the traditional concept of development, which is based on income growth, with the concept of "human development," which also takes into account many other indicators of the quality of life.
4. Cf. Amartya Sen, "Does Business Ethics Make Economic Sense?" in Paul M. Minus, ed., *The Ethics of Business in a Global Economy* (Norwell, MA: Kluwer Academic Publishers, 1993).

businesses whose economic subjects do not regard the satisfactory return on financial resources as their principal objective. Rather, their objective is that of responding to the human needs of those who participate in the business in different ways (including themselves, therefore) and with the various people with whom the business interacts. This attempt is characterized by a double tension: above all, there is the desire to make use of all of the available spaces within the social and economic environment, to obtain these double objectives at the same time. Secondly, there is the desire to make an impact on the general context that surrounds the business, changing the rules that govern the system, thus enabling greater synergy between profitability/competitiveness and social aims. From the perspective of a scholar who studies business economics, three principal questions emerge, which I will attempt to answer in subsequent paragraphs.

What are the characteristics shared by all the Economy of Communion businesses that can form a paradigm for all attempts to create businesses with "ideal motivations"?

What can the Economy of Communion teach us about how one can successfully give rise to entrepreneurship capable of marrying competitiveness and the promotion of the human person and society?

Finally, what challenges will the Economy of Communion businesses have to face if they want to develop in a way that is faithful to the ideal which has begun to inform them?

2.   Paradigmatic Elements of the Business Model under Construction

There are several aspects of the Economy of Communion that could form the cornerstone of any business venture that is motivated by ideal motivations. These can be summarized as follows:

A. Presence within the market economy

B. Attention to the production and to the distribution of wealth
C. Freedom of participation
D. Commitment outside the confines of the business

A. Above all, the experience of the Economy of Communion expresses a will to remain within the institutional, social and economic conditions that condition the lives of everyone, to remain, therefore, within the market economy. The culturally homogeneous industrial estates which have been set up, or will be set up through the project,[5] can be considered as key points of reference for those businesses which take part and not as closed environments into which all the businesses should ideally come together. Evidence of this is found in the fact that the Economy of Communion is found in very diverse sectors (some of which are going through times of profound change) and in a great variety of nations (both industrialized and developing countries, some of which are experiencing profound imbalances).

B. The Economy of Communion wants to have an impact on the moment of *distribution* of wealth, as well as of the moment of *production*. This last point is worthy of great attention. It is not unusual for those motivated by ideals to start up initiatives that aim to create a better redistribution of the wealth that has been produced, and in this way to mitigate against the inequality existing between countries or between different social classes. This emphasis on distribution is typical of those who feel a sense of unease and, more often, a radical sense of distrust toward modernity, based on the intimate conviction that the economic system is grounded on rules that they cannot share. While refusing to work at the heart of the market economy, they prefer to intervene further downstream, in distribution centers, where

5. The idea of the Economy of Communion came about in 1991 on the occasion of Chiara Lubich's visit to the little town of Araceli in Brazil. The little towns—in which groups of people who are part of the Focolare Movement live—were always seen as places that could become models—or in other words—the heart of the new economy. In this way, industrial parks are already under construction near some of the little towns.

they can allay the inevitable injustices produced by those who form the real protagonists of economic and social action.

The Economy of Communion, on the other hand, takes in the whole of the productive sphere and aims to introduce something new at the very heart of economic life. In the experiences of the Economy of Communion one can note numerous innovations in terms of the way that the businesses are run: a change in the orientation of the collaborations in relation to their suppliers and clients, transparency in their relationships with the public administration, a thrust toward innovation (both in terms of product and process) which is sensitive to ecological and human needs of production and consumption, the value placed on every level of worker, the ways that the business is managed under crisis. These last two points are worthy of some further consideration.

In the Economy of Communion businesses, the renewal of the relationship between all those who collaborate in the business is motivated by the conviction, which is already present within business studies, that work constitutes the most important resource at the disposal of the business in view of creating and sustaining a competitive advantage, as well as essential for the development and expression of the person. It is therefore common among the businesses linked to the project to find organizational solutions that encourage everyone to take on responsibility, involvement in the processes of decision-making, due care for health and safety at work, steps to avoid excessive work load, the promotion of an environment which fosters respect, trust and reciprocal praise, and opportunities for formation and continuous learning.

The other aspect where the Economy of Communion demonstrates peculiar features is how it manages in times of crisis. Normally, a time of crisis is one in which the latent differences between people within an organization grow to the point of becoming divisions and conflicts. People increasingly attempt to "abandon ship" before it is too late and external relations tend to become embittered. The Economy of Communion businesses demonstrate radically different phenomena: the crisis brings out the strength of the unity and the cohesion existing among all of the collaborators at different levels. Those outside the business, who have been won over by their trust and respect, moreover, continue to be faithful, even to the point of solidarity through offers of financial assistance.[6] In other words, crisis brings to the fore the presence, and the economic value, of an *intangible asset* which is directly connected to the fact that they participate in the Economy of Communion. The energy for survival and recover comes, in no small part, from those sources.[7]

Moving on to the distribution of wealth within the Economy of Communion, one can see that it is characterized by the criteria laid out in the division of the profits: a third for the poor, while they are in search of work; a third for the formation of "new people," in other words, people who live according to the "culture of giving" that underpins the project; a third for reinvestment in the business. In other words, it is putting forward a very radical ideal. For the individual business people with Economy of Communion businesses, therefore, giving over the means generated by their business would take on the same nature as a donation or sunk capital, even if the money was going to benefit an activity that they regarded as exercising the prerogatives of economic governance.

This type of business, therefore, can be regarded as a particular kind of non-profit organization. In this case, the term non-profit dimension indicates the absence of the objective of distributing eventual profits in an organization that is otherwise governed by the juridical profile and the functional logic typical of other

6. Taking time to develop economic relationships that are reciprocally useful and productive is an integral part of the project, as expressed in an official document: "The business people who adhere to the Economy of Communion are aware of the cultural and political importance that the success of the project could have and help each other at a local and international level, always in a spirit of reciprocal support and solidarity." Besides this help, the business people of the Economy of Communion, when they tell of their experiences, often mention the presence of a "Third Shareholder," whom they call Providence, who makes his presence felt through the coincidence of unexpected positive events.

7. Ever since the beginnings of economic science the "trust factor" has been seen as fundamental to activating and consolidating development. See Salvatore Vicari, "Invisible asset e comportamento incrementale," in *Finanza, Marketing e Produzione,* (1989) and Francis Fukuyama, *Trust.*

productive businesses geared also at recompensing those who invested capital.

C. At this point, however, it is important to underline the fact that the Economy of Communion presents itself as an experience based on *freedom* both in terms of self-determination (the freedom of choice) and in terms of self-fulfillment (the capacity to choose).[8]

The idea of freedom as *self-determination* within the Economy of Communion comes from the fact that each businessperson makes a personal choice to participate in the project, to the extent that his business, personal, and family circumstances allow. In reference to the politics of distribution of profits, which was mentioned above, the following points can be deducted in relation to the principle of freedom:

> The formulation of the principle of the subdivision of profits has changed over time. Initially, the "thirding" of the profits was taken literally, but it has since been regarded as an indicative reference point that has to be adapted to the concrete economic situations in which the businesses find themselves. In the official presentation document about the project in 1998, the rule was presented in the following way: "The businesses have to be managed in ways that will promote the increase of their profits, which the business people freely decide to assign with equal attention to the following: for the growth of the business; to help people in economic difficulty, starting with those who share the culture of giving; and for the diffusion of that culture."[9]

> The criteria by which the distribution of profits takes place is not determined once and for all, but is established year by year by those who govern the business.

8. Stefano Zamagni, "Economia e relazionalitá" (Paper delivered at the conference *Verso un agire economico a misura di persona: la proposta di "Economia di Comunione"* held at the Universitá del Sacro Cuore, Sede di Piacenza, Facoltá di Economia, 29 January 1999).

9. Internal Guidelines for Economy of Communion businesses, New Humanity Bureau of Economy and Labor (April 1998).

As a consequence, the business people are invited to respect the needs that emerge from the life of the business in a given period, for example, the need to finance development.

For those shareholders that do not participate in the Economy of Communion, the normal distribution of their profits quota is respected.

Moving on now to the concept of freedom as self-fulfillment, one has to stress that those who participate in the project say that they are very satisfied and highly motivated to proceed along the path that they have taken. The project is seen as one that corresponds to their deepest needs.[10] Among the businesspeople there is a shared sense that their experience marks the start of a new civilization. This gives them a great commitment to actually make it work and their businesses display a strong sense of vitality and positive vision. The project, moreover, is now exceeding its boundaries and is becoming an important social fact. Other people, who come into contact with it in the world of work, also adhere to the human and religious experience that underpins it.

D. The protagonists of the Economy of Communion also demonstrate another characteristic that is typical of those heads of businesses that have an ideal impetus: they tend to have a *commitment beyond the confines of the business*. Socially committed entrepreneurs do not stay cooped up within their own business but tend to take an interest in the needs around them and in the rules of the game that govern the economic, socio-political system in which they are operating.

---

10. Chiara Lubich affirmed this when she said: "Unlike the consumer economy, which is based on a culture of acquisition, the Economy of Communion is an economy of giving. This might appear difficult, arduous and even heroic, but it is not so: the human person, created in the image of God who is love, finds fulfillment in loving, in giving. Believer and non-believer alike experience this same yearning in the depth of their being. It is this knowledge, born from our experience, that gives us the hope of a universal diffusion of the Economy of Communion" (Lubich, *Economia di Comunione: storia e pensiero* (Rome: Città Nuova, 2001).

This orientation toward extra-business activity has at least two motivations. Firstly, there is a cultural rationale: the same ideal motivation that is at the basis of their style of management guides businesspeople toward taking on board the problems and needs which they meet outside the business. The second reason is a more functional one linked to the development of the organization: entrepreneurs who want to minimize the damage that their business can cause to the environment, for example, could be faced with supplementary costs that more unscrupulous competitors would not have. This could have negative repercussions in terms of profits and competition. If such measures became the norm for all businesses, however, it would be possible to meet the social objective without prejudicing the performance of the business even in the short term. Many scholars of business ethics have underlined the multifaceted nature of the problems associated with the convergence of equity and business interests.[11]

Within the Economy of Communion there are many examples of such initiatives that go beyond the confines of the business: the commitment to respond to the needs of those worst off, the creation of scholarships for the formation of young people destined to work in the world of business, and action to help sustain the development of new businesses.[12]

---

11. Richard T. De George, *Competing with Integrity in International Business* (New York: Oxford University Press, 1993).

12. One of those responsible for the project affirmed: "Through his action in favor of the poor and for the formation of new people, they (the Economy of Communion entrepreneurs) are applying the principle of subsidiarity, carrying out a function in favor of the common good. Civil society is bound to consider them precious friends, sharing their satisfaction when the business is successful. Even if they do not have shares in the company, they will consider it as a social good." Alberto Ferrucci, "Il progetto Economia di Comunione" (Paper delivered at the conference *Verso un agire economico a misura di persona: la proposta di "Economia di Comunione,"* Universitá Cattolica del Sacro Cuore, Sede di Piacenza, Facoltá di Economia, 1999).

3. How a New Way of "Doing Business" Comes about

The Economy of Communion is also of great interest for another reason. Besides being a source of social innovation in business terms, the Economy of Communion project also makes us focus on the conditions—ideas, actions and sequence of actions—by which an enterprise motivated by ideals can go ahead.

History shows us that business ventures that put the needs of people or the common good at the center of their attention seldom rise out of a theoretical deduction. The social doctrine of the Church,[13] on its own, can offer a valuable reference point regarding the criteria and logic underpinning economic action, but it is difficult to see how it can give rise to a phenomenon of mass mobilization within socio-economic realities. Within the Catholic world, discussions over the legitimacy of profit or how to face the dilemmas between innovation and employment, or between sales and damaging publicity, have not borne much fruit. The slow but relentless decline of the experience of the UCID (*Unione Cristiana Imprenditori e Dirigenti*, The Christian Union of Business Entrepreneurs and Executives) in Italy could also be seen as a sign of the inadequacy of this method.[14]

New things come about more through an existing natural process than through deduction. As a result, it is possible to identify the steps through which the Economy of Communion project

---

13. The great social encyclicals of the Catholic Church are: *Rerum Novarum* (Leone XIII, 1891), *Quadragesimo Anno* (Pius XI, 1931), *Mater et Magistra* (John XXIII, 1961), *Populorum Progressio* (Paul VI, 1967), *Octogesima Aveniens* (Paul VI, 1971), *Laborem Exercens* (John Paul II, 1981), *Sollecitudo Rei Socialis* (John Paul II, 1987), *Centesimus Annus* (John Paul II, 1991).

14. The UCID was a major social and economic force in Italy in the post-war era. Two fundamental elements contributed to the success of these types of associations during that time. First, there was a greater vigor within the Catholic world. Second, there was the fight for hegemony on a social and political front between the Christian Democratic tradition and the left-wing forces. It was during these years that groups of the UCID met in many Italian cities, taking in thousands of leaders with businesses of varying sizes and types, and pursuing regular contacts with ministers and high profile personalities. Today the UCID comes across as a worn-out organization, made up of a population of people who are rather old and looked down upon by younger generations, in other words, by the children of the happy protagonists of the post-war era.

was conceived and came into being, aware that similar ideas can also be found in other business initiatives that are sensitive to human and social factors. The evolutionary model that emerges, therefore, is of interest since the basic dynamic through which the businesses motivated by ideals develop, and is not dependent on whether or not the ideal has religious roots.

In order to demonstrate each of the phases identified, I am going to refer to some extracts of the lesson given by Chiara Lubich in the lecture she gave following the conferment of her degree *honoris causa* in Economics at the Catholic University, in Piacenza, Italy.

1. At the origin of every socially innovative enterprise there is a person. You could say, there is an exceptional human presence. On a deeper level, it is difficult to fully explain the nature of this "exceptionality," since it re-proposes the absolute originality that characterizes each person. In order to attempt to explain it, one could put forward the analogy which traditional Western philosophy has defined as "chance," or rather "a superior effect to the sum of the recognized causes."[15] In other words, there are no adequate explanations for the emergence of an entrepreneurial fact that brings profound social innovation. It is only possible to indicate some factors which have, in some way, contributed to generating the phenomenon: up-bringing, a meeting, participation in culturally original and powerful human reality, particular facts that had a great meaning in one's life, working experiences that were particularly informative. In the case of Chiara Lubich, one could speak—in terms that are distinctive within in the Catholic tradition—of the gift of a charism.[16] In the terminology used by organizational studies, one could speak of an institutional leader who is gifted with great

---

15. Boethius, *De Consolatione Philosophiae* V, prose 1, 12–19; Aristotle, *Physics* II, 4–5 and *Nicomachean Ethics*. III, 5.

16. Chiara Lubich herself said of the movement which she founded: "This work . . . is not only human, but of God, of a charism of the Spirit, and for this reason it is so rich and fruitful." Chiara Lubich, "Laurea in economia," 1.

human sensitivity and, hence, the capacity to give rise to a wide consensus and the channeling of much energy.[17]

> The inspiring spark of the Focolare Movement . . . was simple, as the things of God are. During the Second World War that was the fruit of hatred, I had a re-discovery of who God really is: Love. . . . This was the rediscovery that made that first group of young people feel that God was no longer distant, but close by, very close indeed, and present in every circumstance of our life. . . . It was not possible to take anything with us when we ran to the air raid shelters day and night to protect ourselves from the bombs. But we took the gospel, a little gospel, with us. There, during those hours of waiting, reading those words which we already knew, through that special light, we saw them new, unique, universal, made for everyone, eternal, for every age, and made to put into practice. We immediately realized that if they were translated into life, they would bring about a revolution. The world around us, in fact, changed. There are an infinite number of "evangelical episodes" which shower that period. Jesus said to us "Ask and you will receive." . . . We asked for the poor, and every time we were inundated with every kind of thing: bread, powdered milk, jam, wood, and clothes . . . which we took to those who were in need. . . .
>
> The gospel, therefore, was true! God was still keeping his promises.[18]

2. This kind of experience of humanity, as a result of its persuasiveness, tends to spread and begins to involve an ever-growing number of people.

---

17. Phillip Selznick, *Leadership in Administration: A Sociological Interpretation* (Berkeley, CA: University of California Press, 1984).

18. Chiara Lubich, Lecture in Economics, following the conferral of *honoris causa* degree in Economy and Commerce. Università del Sacro Cuore di Milano, Sede di Piacenza, January 31, 1999.

These exultant evangelical experiences spread by word of mouth. Whoever came into contact within this new ecclesial reality that was starting, did not find a movement or even a community. Those who came into contact within it found themselves face to face with—permit me to use a bold but true phrase—Jesus alive in our midst, faithful to his promises.

. . . When the war finished, the Focolare Movement began its rapid expansion first in Italy, and from 1956 onward, throughout Europe, also in the East, and then to the other continents.[19]

3. This phenomenon meets or reveals a need. Faced with this need, it gives rise to the desire or the necessity or the urgency or even the ineluctability of giving an answer. This is the second motivation.

Typical of our movement is the so-called Economy of Communion in freedom, which is a particular experience of social economy. . . .

It came about in Brazil in 1991. The Focolare Movement, which has been present in that nation since 1958, had spread to every state, attracting people from all social classes. For several years, however, despite the communion of goods, I had become aware that—as a result of the growth of the movement . . .—they were unable to cover even the most urgent needs of some of our members. It seemed to me, at that time, that God was calling our movement to do something more, something new.[20]

4. The response outlines the basic features of an ideal image inspired by the novelty that the subject brings. The response, therefore, is a generic one. The details are not well defined, since the practicalities of how to put it into practice are left up those

---

19. Ibid.
20. Ibid.

who will freely bring it about over time. In other words, it is a sketch that in some way identifies the banks through which the entrepreneurial energy could and should flow.

This identification of an ideal image bears a marked resemblance to a characteristic that many management scholars have found in those businesses that are capable of impressive development processes. The most successful companies have come about when there is a leader who is capable of outlining a "business dream,"[21] a "vision"[22] of the future of the organization, which, also on account of its aesthetic value, is able to provide a stable guide for the strategic choices and a deep motivation for those involved.

In this respect, those businesses that are permeated by ideal motivations form a subset of all those businesses that possess a vision of development. This subset is characterized by the fact that this vision, besides involving the prospective productive mission of the business, has to do with what is done with the economic results of the business and to the style of relationship between those who work there and the range of stakeholders.[23] In the case of the Economy of Communion, this ideal image is not generated by the individual businesses, but is proposed by an external factor whose governing principles are shared by the business. In time, through putting this ideal into practice in concrete circumstances (which we will consider further ahead), each business will tend to "personalize" its vision of development, incorporating the character of its main key-actors, as well as the perception that they have of the evolution of the competitive system and the role that their business has to play in this.[24]

---

21. Vittorio Coda, *L'orientamento strategico dell'impresa* (Turin, Italy: UTET Libreria, 1988).

22. James C. Collins and Jerry I. Porras, "Building Your Company's Vision," *Harvard Business Review* (September-October 1996).

23. Mario Molteni, *Alle origine di concezioni innovative di impresa* (Milan, Italy: EGEA, 1990).

24. M. Sellmann, "Economia di Comunione. Alcuni osservazioni empiriche," (Paper delivered at the conference *Verso un agire economico a misura di persona: la proposta di Economia di Comunione* Universitá del Sacro Cuore, Sede di Piacenza, 29 January 1999).

While not being an expert in economic problems, I thought that our people could give rise to businesses, in order to use the talents and resources of everyone so as to produce wealth together to benefit those who are in need. The management of these businesses would have to be entrusted to competent people who would be capable of running them efficiently and produce profits from them. These would have to be shared freely in common. In other words, they would be used for the same goals that the first Christian community had: to help the poor and to give them what they needed to live on so that they could find work. Another part would be used to develop structures for the formation of "new people," . . . that is, people trained and animated by love, who live what we call the "culture of giving." The last part, certainly, would be used to develop the business.[25]

5. The fifth stage, which has no precise time frame, relates to practical experience. As a result of this generic ideal image, each business takes off and pinpoints its precise physiognomy or makes radical changes to it. It is an open dynamic which is largely unpredictable, since it is governed by the impact with the competitive and social environment in which the business is operating. It is also enriched by the possibility of engaging in a comparison with others working for the same objectives: they come across opportunities and problems; solutions emerge; they share experiences and potential solutions; they become involved with other people, and so on.

Many businesses came about as a result of the project and other, existing ones, also participated through modifying their style of business management.[26]

---

25. Chiara Lubich, Lecture in Economics, January 31, 1999.
26. Ibid.

6. The final stage involves reflection on the experience under way. Business studies show that all kinds of innovations (from institutional ones to organizational ones, without exception) mainly come from those who operate in the field.[27] The task of those who are observing and studying, therefore, is to discover the roots of an innovation and to render it accessible so that others can make use of it. The social aims of the businesses also give rise to observable experiences. In time, these will give rise to a new way of doing business that is more sensitive to all the needs of the person and a new way of competing with the other business models present in the competitive context in which they are operating.

This then, in a few words, is the Economy of Communion.

When I proposed it, I certainly did not have a theory in mind. Nonetheless, I can see that it draws the attention of economists, sociologists, philosophers and scholars from other disciplines. While this new experience, and the ideas and categories that underpin it, are rooted in the spirituality of unity, these scholars find reasons to be interested in it that go beyond the Movement in which historically it developed.

In particular, the "Trinitarian" vision of social and interpersonal relationships which is at the basis of the Economy of Communion has enabled some to glimpse a new key that could enrich our understanding of economic interactions and contribute to going beyond the individualistic framework dominant within economic science today.[28]

---

27. The following authors stress the role played by the accumulation of experiences in a business context: David A. Kolb, "On Management and the Learning Process," *Organizational Psychology: A Book of Readings* (New York: Prentice Hall, 1974); Peter M. Senge, *The Fifth Discipline: The Art and Practice of the Learning Organization* (New York: Doubleday, 1994).

28. Chiara Lubich, Lecture in Economics, January 31, 1999.

Figure 1 is a summary of the various stages of development of socially innovative business experience. In particular, the model shows the role that critical reflection on the experience could play in the evolution of the project. Theoretical analysis, in fact, has the following functions:

It contributes to spreading the best practice, identifying particularly efficient solutions, pointing out common mistakes, enabling greater awareness of what is going on, stimulating the commitment of other businesses (feedback process 1);

It can help to modify some of the aspects of the original proposal, with the aim of rendering it more adept to the development of the businesses that are participating (feedback process 2);

It can lead to an increase in the number of people who come into contact and will eventually get involved in the experience that gave rise to the business phenomenon (feedback process 3).

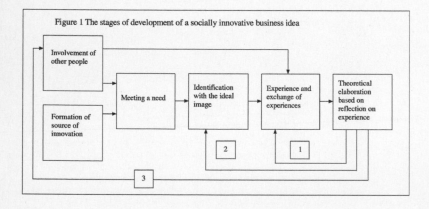

Figure 1 The stages of development of a socially innovative business idea

4. The Challenges of Development

Almost all of the Economy of Communion businesses are small. This has come about as a result of two circumstances. Firstly, those who chose to participate in the project, on the whole, were the owners of small family firms that rarely exceed one hundred employees, or members of groups of co-operatives and non-profit businesses. Alongside these people, there are the new businesses that came about as a result of the project. Since these are still relatively new businesses, they have not yet had the necessary time to grow.

Despite these historical reasons for the small average size of the Economy of Communion businesses, certain questions remain. Is there a place in the Economy of Communion for larger businesses? Is the Economy of Communion formula compatible with development strategies and, above all, rapid growth? One has to admit that if the Economy of Communion were not compatible with such challenges it would be a fundamental limit for the project.

One has to consider, in fact, a characteristic dynamism of every business: it is unable to survive if it is not in continual development. This development is always qualitative, but very often it is also quantitative.[29] Where there is no development, things do not remain stationary—they go backward.

Two factors are necessary for such a situation to arise. The first one is connected to the variable context in which the business finds itself. Businesses today normally operate in a context that is characterized by discontinuity, strongly accelerated changes, and the increased level of internationalization. As a result, those businesses that are static have to face the insistent action of other

---

29. " 'Business development' is . . . understood as a complex phenomenon which consists in a contemporaneous increase in size and quality. In general, this can be observed through an increase in turnover or added value and more generally from an increase in the volume and range of activities carried out. This growth in volume and values in turn gives rise to a growth in quality and the quantity of resources and skills and should give rise to increased results (financial-economic, competitive and social)." Vittorio Coda, "Il problema della continuitá di sviluppo dell'impresa," Giorgio Invernizzi, ed., *Strategie e politica aziendale. La strategia a livello aziendale* (Turin: UTET, 1988).

forces in the competitive system, starting with the action of their direct competitors. The second relevant factor is of an internal nature: in the absence of a tendency toward development, the mental disposition of those at the head of the business becomes institutionalized, the expectations of collaborators are unfulfilled, and internal relations deteriorate. Without creativity and motivation, moreover, the long-term functionality of the business is jeopardized.

It is not my intention here to affirm that the Economy of Communion businesses are condemned to death if they do not become large businesses. There are fields of activity where the small size of the business is a winning feature due to the agility and flexibility that its size allows. But "While this may be true, it is also true that in certain fields and in the presence of certain competitive dynamics, the dimensions of the game play a decisive role since they are linked to the economies of scale, the learning curve and contractual power."[30]

The challenge of development comes to the fore in two particular situations. Firstly, a highly innovative business formula can enable a business to hold such a competitive advantage that it brings about a rapid increase in the rate of demand. Businesses in this situation often find that they are able to grow rapidly as a direct result of the high margins that the innovation has offered. The second situation is where the growth strategy has not been generated by the business itself, but rather, as a result of exogenous forces in the dynamic of the competitive system. If competitors have taken advantage of important economies of scale, for example, this induces other businesses, particularly those that cannot take refuge in a strategy of focalization, to see growth as the only alternative to ceasing their activities.

It is clear, therefore, that consolidation and spread of the Economy of Communion project is closely connected to its capacity not to block, but rather to favor the processes of development of those businesses associated with it. Since the integration of internal and external resources (both monetary and

---

30. Claudio Dematté and Guido Corbetta, eds., *Processi di transizione delle imprese familiari* (Milan, 1993), 89.

non-monetary) is central to development, we can conclude that many of the Economy of Communion businesses will have to face up to a triple challenge:

1. Financial challenge
2. Cultural challenge
3. Strategic challenge

1. Growth presents a *financial challenge*, inasmuch as it normally requires the intake of financial resources which exceed those available for self-financing. Where can the Economy of Communion businesses find such resources? They cannot look to the entrepreneur's family, since participation in the project will have seriously limited the size of the family's wealth. Neither can they look to the other productive businesses that are part of the Economy of Communion, since the lack of capital would be common to all of these businesses. A possible answer could come from the financial societies that are beginning to emerge within the Economy of Communion with the aim of channeling resources through loans or shares in the businesses taking part.[31] This is a source, however, which has so far proved to have limited potential.[32]

The only remaining solution is for the Economy of Communion to turn to external sources of financing. At least two possible scenarios can be imagined. Firstly, one could imagine a situation in which entities (both people and juridical entities) with financial resources are struck by the ideal commitment of those at the helm of an Economy of Communion business. As a result, they decide to invest in it, renouncing their expectation of either all or part of the return on their investment. It is right to think, however, that this would not provide a stable source of funding.

---

31. Benedetto Gui, "Impresa ed Economia di Comunione. Alcuni riflessioni," *Nuova Umanitá* XIV (March-June 1992): 80–81.
32. One could also consider the possibility of linking up with others who are promoting so-called "ethical investment," which is currently in a phase of rapid expansion.

One has to turn, therefore, to potential investors who would be seeking a return on their capital, admitting the fact that it is not necessary for all the shareholders to adhere to the tripartite distribution of profits suggested by the project. In this way, they would not have to exclude the involvement of those who have a positive view of the development plan of the business and who, perhaps as a result of their esteem for the Economy of Communion, would like to turn the competitive advantage which businesses within the project have access to, to their own personal advantage. The introduction of these shareholders who expect a return, moreover, would ensure that the Economy of Communion businesses do not remain outside the dynamics of the financial market. It is not, therefore, an easy way to follow, also due to the implications which are discussed below.

2. The development of the business in terms of dimensions, the opening up to investors who do not fully share the ideals of the Economy of Communion and the increase in the number of collaborators (who will not be culturally homogeneous, above all in situations where the rapid growth of the business prevents careful selection from a motivation point of view), will present a big *cultural challenge*.[33] Remaining faithful to the origins of the project in such a situation, on the one hand, requires lots of imagination and a high degree of freedom within the structures initially put in place. On the other hand, it demands a continual renewal of the commitment to the ideal, since the intense

---

33. The following declaration of an exponent of the Economy of Communion shows how difficulties faced in relation to the development of the dimensions of the business can even lead to the opportunities for business development being jeopardized: "The new challenge faced by the Economy of Communion businesses in the Philippines is the challenge of how to raise the capital to finance growth. The Rural Ibaan Bank, for example, has seen a rapid increase in deposits and now, according to the rules of the Central Bank, they are risking undercapitalization. In order to reach the necessary level of investment new shareholders will have to enter. These shareholders, however, if they do not adhere to the Economy of Communion, could undo everything. Moreover, if the bank becomes bigger, it would not perhaps be possible to rely on a sufficient number of 'new people' to offer the same services as it offers today. Our main challenge is *how to form many new people for our businesses*." Tita Puangco, "Lo sviluppo delle aziende nelle Filippine," *Economia di Comunione* III, 1–2 (April–July 1997): 8–9.

commitment to the business and the concerns connected with it could lead to the gradual or sudden abandonment of the initial inspiration in order to embrace the normal business logic as an end in itself.

This challenge has to be faced. Otherwise, the desire to remain faithful to the ideal could lead the entrepreneurs to "play safe" and adopt an attitude of keeping their businesses small out of fear—perhaps not explicitly—that the noble aim for which the business came about could be lost.

In this way, the Economy of Communion could see the development of a phenomenon that is common to businesses within family control. In these businesses, out of fear of losing the total control, the leaders renounce opportunities to grow and to develop alliances, which would bring in new shareholders. Such attitudes, moreover, are not necessarily demonstrated in saying "no" to a proposal. Even prior to this, they are manifest in a lack of interest in searching for new possibilities, in interpreting changes in the sector as threats to the business rather than opportunities, in regarding a process of gradual concentration as something inherently bad—the show of strength of stronger players—and not as a stimulus for greater efficiency. If one substitutes the egoistic objectives of the family with the ideals that characterize those who work for the Economy of Communion, the same mistake could occur from a business perspective.

3. This leads on to the third challenge: the *strategic challenge*. In many sectors, in order to stay in the market, to grow, it is necessary to establish close alliances with others who are carrying out similar or complementary activities. This step further exacerbates the cultural problems that have already been pointed out. It is rare for business partners to be bearers of the kinds of ideal motivations that the Economy of Communion business people hold. The need to create strategic alliances, therefore, means adopting organizational and management logics that are less in keeping with the logic of the Economy of Communion. This too could present the entrepreneur with the difficult challenge of trying to stick to the original goal.

5. Conclusion

The various challenges that have been mentioned here mean that those who participate in the Economy of Communion have their work cut out for them. This is true on two fronts.

Above all, it will be necessary to critically reflect often on the guiding principles that were established or rather, on their formulation. In other words, as the experience grows, it will be necessary to identify which general indications can best fulfill the ideals for which the project came about. The primary means to bring about this first stage of translation into practice, therefore, is through reflecting on experience.

The second level regards the individual businesses. Given the range of competitive environments, nations and types of people involved, solutions will have to be tailored and original. Faithfulness to the goals of the project will mean each entrepreneur will have to use all his imagination to come up with the most suitable institutional, organizational and strategic solutions.

In order to reach an efficient solution to these challenges, therefore, mere adherence to a predetermined organizational form is not enough. It will require the idealistic and critical commitment of all the subjects involved. The three challenges cannot be resolved, moreover, on the basis of a shrewd theory. They have to be addressed by facing the problems in the field through entrepreneurial creativity, managerial professionalism and the constant growth of a strong ideal motivation.

In order to address this double task, those who work for the Economy of Communion will be able to draw on the valuable collaboration of universities and other research and training institutes. These entities, through people who are sympathetic to the ideals of the Economy of Communion, can act as reference points and comparisons so as to evaluate the evolutionary trajectory of the project, the factors influencing the diffusion of ideas and the most efficient solutions that they have developed. The protagonists of the Economy of Communion can expect help from those involved in the world of economic and business research, enabling them to be more creative and attentive to the problems that they will face as they grow.

✧ Productive Organizations with Ideal Aims and Personal Fulfillment: Interpersonal Relations and Horizons of Meaning[1]

Benedetto Gui
University of Padova, Italy

In his paper, McCloskey[2] caused a stir by talking of "economic rhetoric" and claiming that the objective pretext of this science does not correspond to the facts. If this is the state of play, it is better to lay my cards on the table and to tell you straight away which side of this rhetorical exercise, this "economic sermon" is on. I will try to focus attention on two particular "dimensions" of personal fulfillment. They are two dimensions which the normal lenses used to examine the economy do not allow us to focus on, but upon which both the organization of economic activity and the dominant culture within this subsystem of social life have a powerful influence. I am talking about the quality of personal relationships and—something even more difficult to express with the language of economics—the intrinsic meanings that inform our actions as entrepreneurs, workers, and consumers. I will then try to show that all of the above are very relevant to those economic organizations that have ideal aims and, in particular, to the Economy of Communion project.

Given that the importance of interpersonal relationships has received some more attention within economic literature, I will

1. This paper is a reworking of one I presented at the conference *I risvolti economici delle relazioni interpersonali* promoted by the Lanza Foundation in the context of the *Salone dell'Economia Sociale e Civile "Civitas"* (Padova, April 1997). I would like to thank Luigino Bruni and Ottorino Chillemi for their fruitful discussions and useful suggestions.
2. David N. McCloskey, "The Rhetoric of Economics," *Journal of Economic Literature* 21 (2) (1983): 481–517.

discuss this a bit more at length. This does not mean, however, that the question of meaning is of secondary importance.

1.   The Economy and Interpersonal Relations

1.1   An imaginary (but not too imaginary) situation

Imagine that you have just found the house of your dreams. It is in a lovely square with lots of grass, with that extra room you were hoping for and it is close to the highway that goes straight to your office. You buy it. Then little by little you realize that the neighbors are impossible to live with: the one upstairs screams all the time, the one next door who when you asked if you could borrow an egg to make some mayonnaise told you to mind your own business and stop disturbing others. It is not possible, more-over, to let the children play safely in the neighborhood. The only social group is a gang of delinquents who hang out on the corner smoking: this means that you have to resign yourself to accom-panying your children to the other side of town every afternoon so that they can play sports or music. During weekends, if you haven't made arrangements to meet up with an old friend, there is no possibility of meeting up with some neighbors, so you have to get in the line of traffic and head for the hills, just for the sake of doing something. Your grandmother, who lives with you, is also dissatisfied: apart from the neighbors (whom we have already mentioned), there is no meeting place nearby that can be reached on foot. Although there is a beautiful public park in the area, it is not advisable to go there alone since some incidents have taken place there and the grass is littered with syringes left by drug addicts. The local library, although well lit and well stocked, is not used very often and is certainly not somewhere you would go to meet new people. And it is not even worth talking about shops where people can meet each other: everyone goes to the mall in the suburbs, but finds different people there every time, and nobody seems to have time to talk!

The school that you chose for your children is nothing to laugh about either. The building is modern and the cleaning company is doing its job at keeping it clean, the teachers are well-trained, there is also a computer lab with the latest equipment. The real problem, however, is the atmosphere inside: students make fun of those who make mistakes or those who are not dressed in the latest fashion and they carry out not very amusing pranks, while the parents you have tried to talk to are anxious above all to say that their children would never do things like that and that it is all the fault of this one or that one who is ill-mannered. It would be highly unlikely that you could arrange for the parents to start a carpool for bringing those children who live on the same street to school! The result is that every morning it is a battle to convince the children to go to school because they don't want to, and getting them to do their homework each afternoon is a pain for the whole family.

When it comes to work, you have a secure job in a large company that pays a good salary and does not require excessive commitment. But here too, there is not a pleasant atmosphere: colleagues are constantly backstabbing, those in charge of the different offices do not agree with each other (with the risk that if you obey the orders of one you risk being told off by the other), and the new director treats everyone as if he or she were rubbish, so much so that one of your colleagues is already having a nervous breakdown!

1.2 Is something missing?

The aim of this long series of more or less realistic circumstances is to give rise to or reinforce a doubt that the reader who has patiently reached this far may have. Is there something missing from our accounts?

While the unfortunate protagonists of the saga that I described would never think to describe their situation as "well-being," every economic measure of their *ménage* would be highly positive: they have a good income; they are the owners of valuable property; they enjoy high levels of private consumption (which include all the afternoon activities for their children, quite likely making use of two cars) and high levels of public consumption (which are valued as costs—we mentioned the school, park, library, and roads, which all have a high cost according to the description). It is likely that the indicators for the piece of the economic system which surrounds the family in question will also be high: malls, sports clubs, music schools, to which we can also add car mechanics and garages. One could cast doubt on the economic results of the business where our protagonist works, if it is true that within it there are such tense relationships. It is possible, however, that the effects of this will not be seen so much in today's accounts as in the future.

The number of inadequacies of the indicators of economic well-being normally in use is in some ways inevitable. Some scholars and commentators have been working on these for some time. I will mention two: consumption can have a defensive nature (think about the cost of reinforced fences, security alarms and so on), through which we risk interpreting higher spending with a higher level of satisfaction. Secondly, as the ecological movement has quite rightly underlined, calculations of income, consumption, and Gross National Product, do not subtract environmental costs (the deterioration of the natural environment and the exhaustion of non-renewable natural resources), and hence, we tend to overvalue the benefits of economic activity.

What I would like to underline here, however, is another inefficiency of normal accounting, which is even more inadequate than those mentioned above: such calculations do not take into account the sphere of relationships, or what we could call the "human/social environment," in any way.

Every deficiency in calculating inevitably comes back to, as a cause or effect, a lack of attention to the phenomenon itself: insufficient capacity to recognize it, understand it or conceptualize it. An important example of this, which can be added to the one cited above in relation to environmental goods, could be seen in the recent history of the Soviet Union and other countries that had planned economies. The materialist cultural tradition, which focused completely on tangible goods (coal, steel, ones which you can measure in tons, in other words), gave less importance to immaterial services (consultancy, commercial mediation, financial services, restoration, personal service, etc.), which now represent the leading sector in the most advanced economies. Proof of this can be found in the fact that the most used economic indicator in the USSR was gross (or net) material product, which excluded a great part of the services industry. It should not be surprising, then, that when the communist systems collapsed, people became aware that the services sector was more underdeveloped than the others.

In the same way, in Western societies, up till now there has been a lack of attention to the dimension of informal relations between citizens and, in particular, a lack of understanding of the part that they play in economic affairs. By saying this, I would like to free us from a common misunderstanding in this area. Hearing us talk of the economic consequences of interpersonal relationships could seem dangerous or even offensive precisely for those who are most sensitive to this dimension of personal and social life that we associate more with gratuity than calculations. In fact, there could seem to be the risk that these relationships could also be caught up in the sphere of self-interested exchanges, commercial rationality, and therefore, become contaminated. On the other hand, if we think that economic science is guided by the search for happiness, even before being the search for material wealth, it is rather strange for it to exclude important dimensions of well-being (an expression which does not mean "high levels of consumption"). Naturally, it is necessary to bear in mind the special qualities of this kind of "good," and how they are created and can be destroyed. We will consider this further ahead.

I would like to underline several points relating to the economic consequences of interpersonal relationships. Firstly, informal relationships have an important bearing on the well-being of the members of a community, whether directly or through the influence that they have on the development of economic activities. Secondly, informal relationships are influenced by individual and collective decisions, which ought to be taken into consideration within economic expertise, but economic science lacks adequate concepts to describe these influences in the "relational" sphere (and far less the capacity to offer advice on how to manage them better). I will now try to develop these two statements.

1.3   Social capital, relational goods, and related ideas

Here and there in the scientific literature, there are signs that the theme of the economic aspects of informal relationships between citizens is of interest to an increasing number of social scientists, and also economists. Articles on the subject, some of which have yet to be published, have begun to circulate. In some of these articles there is an attempt to try to adapt the language of economic theory to tackle the question of relationships through introducing new concepts, some of which are mentioned above: *social capital* and *relational goods*.

Of these concepts, the one which has been most developed is "social capital"—for that reason we have included it in the title. James Coleman writes: *"Social capital* is created when the relations between people change in a way that facilitates action."[3] He continues: *"Social capital* is defined by its function. It is not a singular entity, but a variety of different entities which share two characteristics: they all consist in some aspect of the social structure, and they facilitate certain actions of individuals within those structures."[4]

The definition of social capital itself is therefore focused on the idea that the networks of informal relationships between citizens—or rather the characteristics of these networks—have tangible economic effects, which can be compared, for example, to a road (a capital good in this case) which facilitates commercial activity. In each case we are clearly talking about capital public goods that benefit a large number of people.

---

3. James S. Coleman, *Foundations of Social Theory* (Cambridge, MA: Belknap Press, 1990), 304.

4. Coleman, *Foundations of Social Theory*, 302.

Some examples will help to make this point clearer.

The speed of diffusion of new therapies is dependent, to a great extent, on the intensity of the network of informal relationships between doctors.

The social norm, which is present in some societies but not all, by which adults who see children in dangerous situations feel called to intervene, is very valuable for parents, as it means that their children can play outside unsupervised.

In some countries, the breakdown of trust between doctors and patients has led to the growth of lawsuits brought by patients who are dissatisfied with the service they have received. This, in turn, has led to an increase in the cost of treatment, and in some cases, the refusal of surgeons to treat relatives of lawyers.

The Grameen Bank has managed to give loans at a very low interest rate to artisans and poor farmers living in Bangladesh. The rate of default on repayments has been very low, especially considering that in this country the phenomenon of default on loans constitutes an enormous problem for normal banking activities, giving a great advantage to loan sharks. The key to this noteworthy success is the innovative system through which loans are given to groups that are responsible for selecting the borrowers, motivating the repayments, and controlling who is offered a loan within the village community. In other words, this innovative development bank relies heavily on the close-knit network of relationships between the inhabitants in the rural areas.[5]

People are beginning to say that certain elements of social capital, like the diffusion of the behavioral norms of collaboration, respect for the social norms and the cultural predisposition to trust (and to be trusted by) administrators outside one's immediate family circle, are important preconditions for

---

5. Timothy Besley, "Nonmarket Institutions for Credit and Risk Sharing," *Journal of Economic Perspectives* 9 (3) (1995): 115–127.

economic development—in particular in relation to the flour-
ishing of large private organizations.[6]

It is worth repeating that what has been said so far regards
normal situations and people who are in many ways representa-
tive of a large swath of the population. This prudential choice has
the advantage of demonstrating how these problems are of
general interest. In fact, if we had focused our attention on situations where there is particular unease, the importance of these
social networks would be even clearer. In particular, access to
collaboration (or even just communication) with other people is
an invaluable resource for elderly people who are no longer
self-sufficient or without family, for people with disabilities, for
poorly socialized children and for disadvantaged families (with
very limited chances of finding solutions on their own to the
problems they face).

The other expression I mentioned, relational goods, is less well
defined. It has been utilized in English economic literature by
Carole Uhlaner,[7] who attempts to use the terminology of individual rationality to explain very important phenomena like
political participation, which involves a high level of costs and
the apparent absence of advantages. The author comes to the
conclusion that in this case, as in many others, what the individual gains is the enjoyment of immaterial goods, like a sense of
belonging to a group, a sense of identity, approval from other
people. Moreover, the goods in question here "can only be
enjoyed if shared with the others," and hence, constitute a
particular kind of public good.

My reflection on this topic[8] started by considering another
example of relational goods—that patrimony of shared knowledge, experiences, desire to collaborate—which links a group of

---

6. Francis Fukuyama, *Trust.*
7. Carole Uhlaner, " 'Relational Goods' and Participation: Incorporating Sociability
   into a Theory of Rational Action," *Public Choice* 62 (1989): 253–285.
8. Benedetto Gui, "Economia e 'fioritura umana,' " Stefano Zamagni, ed., *Economia,
   democrazia, istituzioni in una societá in trasformazione* (Bologna, Italy: Il Mulino,
   1997) 53–80; and "Interpersonal Relations: A Disregarded Theme in the Debate
   on Ethics and Economics," Alan Lewis and Karl-Erik Warneryd, eds., *Ethics and
   Economic Affairs* (London: Routledge, 1994).

neighbors together. This patrimony is very rarely recognized as such, and, as a result, is under threat from the owner's decisions, for example, to modify the use of an area. This would have consequences if the current occupiers were eventually able to afford to buy part of the property. Since they were unable to control whether other occupiers stayed or not, they would risk seeing that extra value, which came from maintaining the current composition of occupiers, being wasted. Other examples of relational goods are: the habit of meeting up on certain occasions and the familiarity which exists within a group of friends or relatives, a good whose values is well understood by those who have had to go to live in a new city; well-established associations which run activities supported by members linked together by mutual acquaintance and trust.

Finally, I would like to mention another concept which is closely related to those being considered here, but which refers to a particular kind of relationship which we have not mentioned up till now: the relationship between those working within the same business. Among these people, a "team human capital" can be generated, which consists of the habit of collaborating, a specialized language in use within the group, an ability to gauge the reactions colleagues may have to an unexpected difficulty, knowledge of the specific talents of each one in what they are doing. In other words, there is "mutual understanding."[9]

This part of the paper, dedicated to definitions, has enabled us, above all through examples, to offer an initial answer to the original question regarding the effects of interpersonal relations on the well-being of citizens. We have considered the direct effects they can have on the quality of life, as well as the indirect impact that relationships can have on the development of specifically economic activities.

We will now move on to the second question, which to some extent has a bearing on the first one. It regards the effects that decisions made in the sphere of political economy and economic

---

9. Benedetto Gui and Otterino Chillemi, "Team Human Capital and Worker Mobility," *Journal of Labor Economics* 15 (4) (1997).

mechanisms have on the networks of relationships among citizens.

1.4 The effects of the economy and political economy on interpersonal relationships

Economic life has always been a privileged source of opportunities to build relationships (between commercial contacts, between colleagues, between shareholders). The workings of the economic system, however, can also have negative repercussions on the structure of relationships. In particular, they can lead to excessive mobility, the desire to work too hard, which reduces the time given over to building relationships, and through the advertising industry, the diffusion of a competitive culture, not only between businesses, but between individuals (in terms of career, consumption, social life) too. A recurring motive is that goods in the sphere of relationships are like public goods and it is well known that private economic activities tend to exploit these for their own ends, with the result that they deteriorate.[10]

Both public and private decisions that relate to the structure of commerce, town planning, the school system, working hours, occupational and geographical mobility[11] all have repercussions for the maintenance and creation of networks of social relationships. What is lacking, however, is a conceptual framework within which the repercussions of these relationships can be understood and valued in decision-making with the same weight given to the repercussions traditionally understood as economic ones, for which there are well-established quantifiable procedures. As a result, the effects on social relations tend to be ignored or at best given little consideration, with the risk that relationships are being systematically penalized.

---

10. See, for example, Stefano Zamagni, ed., *Economia, democrazia, istituzioni in una società in trasformazione* (Bologna: Il Mulino, 1997), 147–148.
11. See Maurice Schiff, "Social Capital, Labor Mobility, and Welfare: The Impact of Uniting States," *Rationality and Society* 4 (2) (1992): 157–175.

As if to make things more difficult, as Yew-Kwang Ng[12] observed, there is the fact that the creation of relationships cannot be directly subsidized or otherwise encouraged. Doing this could lead to the relationships themselves becoming distorted, since a degree of spontaneity and a lack of ulterior motives are two important conditions for good relationships. The only possible way of encouraging this, it seems, would be through indirect policies that encourage activities where such relationships can flourish (for example, the pedestrianization of meeting places like town squares, supporting retail outlets in easily accessible places, and so on).

Taking the relational dimension into account in the traditional economic vision, in which mutual advantage is reached through the market, taxes and subsidies if each one takes care of their own interests, leads to another reason for perplexity. Here, in fact, there are important public goods whose creation and maintenance require gratuity and the capacity for all those involved to be open to the others. This requires a culture that is saturated with authentic relationships, in the search for not personal success, but true fulfillment as a person.

When the capacity to collaborate and establish relationships is recognized as an important ingredient in the creation and maintenance of these public goods, education about how to develop these capacities has to be seen as just as important in the productive environment as gaining technical and organizational skills. Such a capacity is recognized in modern theories of development as "investment in human capital," and is seen as the principal task of public authorities. It is necessary, therefore, to widen and correct this definition of what is productive and, hence, what constitutes human capital.

---

12. Yew-Kwang Ng, "Non-Economic Activities, Indirect Externalities and Third-Best Policies," *Kyklos* 28 (3) (1975): 507–525.

2. Economy and Intrinsic Meanings

The other dimension of personal fulfillment that economic reflection finds it hard to take into account, since it is even more difficult to define and quantify, but not less important for this reason, is the fact that we live in a universe of meanings and find ways of attaching intrinsic—rather than merely instrumental—meanings to what we do. With the exception of a few,[13] the great majority of economists up until a few years ago shared the dominant opinion—which then became a widespread way of thinking—that this dimension had nothing to do with the sphere of economic life and that the only task of the economy was to supply people, resources and the means through which each one could pursue his or her own life.

The implications of this vision of reality are all too evident. One could argue, clearly, that the justification for leaving the theme of intrinsic meanings attached to actions out of the analysis is a useful simplification that facilitates our understanding of the essential phenomena of the economy. In reality, however, this simplification has often proved to be misleading. On the one hand, from a positivist point of view, economic science has found that it is incapable of understanding certain important phenomena.[14] On a normative level, on the other hand, it has come up with counterproductive prescriptions. A typical example is that of monetary incentives within businesses. In many cases, such incentives have been shown to represent the

---

13. For example, Hirschman invited economists to take into account that certain activities, which he calls *non-instrumental* are not undertaken in view of enjoying a result so much as out of a search for meaning and identity. Albert O. Hirschman, "Against Parsimony: Three Easy Ways of Complicating Some Categories of Economic Discourse," *American Economic Review* 74 (2) (1984): 89–96. Kolm, moreover, underlined that an economic system cannot be judged only on its consumable *output* that enables purchasing power, but also the intrinsic value attached to the interactions within the system. Serge-Christrophe Kolm, "The Theory of Reciprocity and of the Choice of Economic Systems: An Introduction," *Investigaciones-Economicas* 18 (1) (1994): 67–95.

14. For example, the willingness to pay more for public goods than what is strictly necessary; see Daniel Kahneman and Jack L. Knetsch, "Valuing Public Goods: The Purchase of Moral Satisfaction," *Journal of Environmental Economics and Management* 22 (1) (1992): 57–70.

most effective weapon precisely because introducing or strengthening an "extrinsic" motivation (normally of a monetary nature) can displace the intrinsic motivation (inner satisfaction in contributing to something in line with the workers' values). The result is that a deeply held and valued commitment to the final result is transformed into instrumental collaboration which only looks for the immediate measurable result recognized by the incentive scheme.[15] If this is true, then one needs to recognize that, here too, as in all of the other aspects of personal life, there is a mixture of instrumental and "expressive" logic.[16]

3. Interpersonal Relations, Horizons of Meaning, and Businesses with Ideal Aims

Before continuing, I would like to point out that since relationality and the search for meaning are universal needs, they exist to some extent in every human context, including the sphere of commerce and production, as confirmed in the vast literature on occupational psychology. Nevertheless, individual incentives and the dominant culture both contribute to making instrumentality prevalent in actions and in relationships.

One of the main challenges faced by productive organizations with ideal aims is precisely that of showing how it is possible to work for human fulfillment on these two more subjective dimensions, also in the world of production and the market. Even for those who try to manage a business for the common good, rather than simply to serve their personal interests, the first dimensions

---

15. Many economists have taken an interest in this in recent years. See, for example, Bruno S. Frey, *Not Just for Money: An Economic Theory of Personal Motivation* (Cheltenham, UK: Edward Elgar Publishing, 1997); David M. Kreps, "Intrinsic Motivation and Extrinsic Incentives," *American Economic Review* 87 (2) (1997): 359–364; and Robert Gibbons, "Incentives in Organizations" (Working Paper: National Bureau of Economic Research [NBER] no. 6695, 1998).

16. Certain authors have sought to enlarge the concept of rationality used in economic theory so as to introduce the possibility that some actions can be justified not so much by their effects—on the basis of the traditional consequentialist approach—as on the value which the agent affirms through his or her action or in the search for meaning and identity which the action permits. See Hargreaves-Heap, *Rationality in Economics*.

of human fulfillment which come into relief are those of having and doing, which are in some ways specifically tied to the sphere of economic action.[17] These include objectives such as the creation and distribution of wealth and the creation of jobs for those in need. The availability of material goods is an important condition, even if not the only one, in defining what the Nobel Prize winner Amartya Sen calls "capability."[18] He defines this as the possibility to carry out a whole range of "functions" (such as eating healthily, keeping well, knowing and expressing oneself effectively, carrying out a meaningful role in society, choosing what one does in life); carrying out a professional task within economic life, even apart from the income that it may bring, is a privileged expression of one's potential and ability to take on responsibility. It is not by chance, then, that all forms of business management both in the past and in the present, which explicitly propose to change society according to certain ideals, have tried to bring about a more just distribution of income and access to work than the one that takes place within the market, through public organizations and through the informal norms of allocation associated with families and communities. We could think of the different kinds of cooperatives, which adopt rules of profit distribution and fix prices in a different way to that normally followed in the economic system. Another example, where this is even more evident, are those non-profit organizations which, as their name suggests, do not distribute profits and fix their prices in favor of the services that they offer to certain categories of people (for example, reduced rents for families with low incomes or child care for large families). Yet another example is the job creation schemes where creating job opportunities for people who have been disadvantaged in one way or another is the main objective.

To provide answers to the questions posed by the relational dimension and non-instrumental meanings is, in some ways, the new frontier facing productive organizations with ideal aims

---

17. Benedetto Gui, "Economia e 'fioritura umana.'"
18. Amartya Sen, *Inequality Reexamined* (Boston, MA: Harvard University Press, 1995).

and also their strong point. In fact, on the one hand, the elimination (or at least the weakening) of the profit motive weakens the conflicts of interest that surround the organization's activities, removing an obstacle to the creation of a human environment imbued with gratuity. On the other hand, having the chance to get involved in something, not for personal interest in exchange for adequate pay, but in order to promote valid objectives which are meaningful in themselves (clearly, for those who share them), leads to much greater horizons of meaning in which to situate one's action.

Up till now we have discussed the objective elements that characterize these organizations. Onto these, moreover, the business culture they chose to create (and manage) is grafted. It is not for nothing, for example, that the cooperative movement has always felt the need to define itself not only in terms of practices which promote participation and solidarity, but also in terms of the adoption of a particular culture and, therefore, corresponding formation courses. One can see that the capacity of productive organizations with ideal aims to create a context that favors the creation of positive interpersonal relations and the manifestation of intrinsic motivations is also one of the conditions for their objective success. For example, those who are dedicated to the recuperation of vulnerable people by inserting them into the workplace, recognize that it is essential not only to be able to offer them a job and a wage, but also a welcoming and involving social environment, that is, one that is capable of supplying the new task with deeper motivations.

All of this is particularly relevant for the businesses that are part of the Economy of Communion. In fact, they define themselves, on the one hand, through the commitment of their owners to earmark part of their profits for goals that are also shared by other *stakeholders* (first of all their workers, but also their clients and suppliers). On the other hand, they define themselves through their commitment to the "culture of giving," and more precisely, to a kind of giving which is certainly characterized by gratuity, but at the same time is open to reciprocity, or in other words, to a profound meeting which is substantially based on equality, suggested by the word "communion" (the spread of that culture constitutes one of the destinations of the profits outside the business, alongside providing immediate assistance to those who find themselves in need). It is no coincidence, then, that one of the effects most readily cited by those who have become involved in the project is creation of a positive human environment within the business, which favors personal development in the widest sense. For these businesses, maintaining a human environment marked by attention for the other, whether a colleague nearby or a beneficiary far away, is not so much a desirable by-product of their desire to share their profits according to the goals mentioned above, as a parallel objective which is just as important and actively pursued. This observation also re-proposes another recurring theme in the testimonies of those responsible for the businesses participating in the project: the desire to be faithful to a style which prioritizes openness and attention to each person met face-to-face in the course of carrying out economic activities. This can be seen in their readiness to renounce a part of their expected profits—or more precisely, taking on this risk—if this is what "creating communion" requires. A typical situation where this comes to the fore is where an employer is faced with an employee whom it would be advisable to sack, if he were following the standard norms of society. Instead, he decides to take the risk of trusting him in order to avoid marginalization, and in the end finds him to be a valuable resource. In another situation, it may be that one entrepreneur is willing to proceed with a commercial relationship with a supplier despite a past episode in which the merchandise he delivered did not tally with that agreed upon. In this case, he did it out of solidarity rather than a calculation, since otherwise the supplier would face an economic collapse he did not deserve. Or finally, it could be reflected in the willingness of an entrepreneur to put aside a brilliant idea that has not been understood, which eventually leads to him winning the esteem of a manager who later offers his full collaboration on the idea.

4.   Conclusions

The goods that economics have to deal with, therefore, are not as obvious as one could think. The answer is at least in part historically and culturally determined. But I would go further. It seems that it is possible to say that over time, there has been a certain correspondence between public opinion in favor of the various organizational forms of economic activities—the market guided by the profit motive, public supplies, and private supplies with motives other than profit—and the attention economic science has given to three large categories of goods. The emphasis placed on the market in reconciling the aims of individual profit and the common good at the end of the nineteenth and the beginning of the twentieth century, was accompanied by greater attention to those material goods that are privately consumed (alongside a description of markets as perfect competition). The great question of public intervention in the economy which dominated the central part of the twentieth century corresponded with greater attention to public goods and the public effects of private choices—on the one hand, this regarded the macroeconomic externalities that one's choice to spend would have on the employment and selling opportunities of the others and, on the other hand, the microeconomic externalities, for example, those regarding the environment. All of this resulted in an excessive optimism about the capacity of public organizations to be faithful to the instruments of the common good. The attention which is today given to businesses with ideal aims, among which there is the Economy of Communion, goes hand in hand with the growth of interest in another type of good—or rather, other dimensions of personal fulfillment—which seem increasingly urgent: the insertion of a network of positive interpersonal relationships and involvement in meaningful activities.

I would like to conclude by observing that when we speak of "economy of the whole person" or "economy for the person" it is true that we are asking economic organizations to take care of the other needs of those involved (needs which would be otherwise overlooked so as to obtain economic benefits). At the same time, however, widening this vision also gives rise to added resources—those in the ideal, moral and relational spheres —which, as the history of many businesses in the Economy of Communion show, can become crucial factors in business success.

✧ On the Foundation and Meaning of the "Economy of Communion" Experience

Stefano Zamagni
University Of Bologna, Italy

I will attempt to respond to a question that has two sides. On the one hand, what is it that characterizes, and hence determines the unique function of the Economy of Communion in a post-industrial society like the one we live in today? On the other hand, what challenges does the uplifting experience of the Economy of Communion present to standard economic theory, and more generally, to the economic sciences and social sciences? I am not concerned here, due to the limited space available, to outline the way in which the Economy of Communion businesses operate. Others have done this earlier in this volume. Neither am I concerned with retracing the philosophical and theological foundation of this experience, even if this has to be done urgently and courageously. It is not possible, in fact, to simply say that the Economy of Communion represents a mere fruit of the stage of maturity of the Focolare Movement. This would be a very reductive way of looking at what is an intriguing "sign of the times."

1. Before responding to the above questions, I think it would be appropriate to clarify a common misunderstanding—the tendency to confuse gratuity with reciprocity. In order to clarify the profound difference between these two concepts, one needs to refer specifically to the field of voluntary work where this confusion tends to generate the most serious consequences. As is well known, the widespread opinion among "insiders" is that the foundational value governing voluntary action is gratuity.

My position with respect to this, instead, is that while it may be true that gratuity is the *modus operandi* of volunteering, what distinguishes it from other forms of human action is the production of values within social ties. In that way, the specific goal of voluntary action is the generation of strong links of relationality among people; its method, i.e., its way of reaching that goal, is gratuity.

Why is it important to distinguish between the "goal" and "method"?[1]

There are three main reasons. Firstly, if we reduced the essence of volunteering to gratuity alone, how would we distinguish it from philanthropy? Philanthropists also give gratuitously, that is, they donate to others. But these kinds of gestures hardly ever give rise to relationality in the true sense of the word. In fact, philanthropy, like altruism, is a virtue that is perfectly compatible with individualism. The problem with many types of altruism that we see at work in our daily lives is that they represent *altruism without the other*. Hence, they run the risk of having those perverse effects that Seneca reminds us of in his tenth letter to Lucilio: "Human madness has reached the point where doing big favors for someone has become very dangerous: he, in fact, because he regards it as shameful not to return this exchange, would like to remove his creditor. There is no greater hatred than that which is born from the shame of having betrayed a benefice."

This brings me to the second reason. If we reduce voluntary action to gratuity only, we will never be able to fully appreciate its specific added value. What is distinctive about voluntary action, is that the "practices of caring" in which the culture of giving is manifest, come about not only *for* the others but *with* them. It is said that dolphins also freely come to the aid of other animals that are apparently of different species. Such behavior, however, does not constitute relationality, since that means taking into consideration the personal identity of the other. In reality, at the

---

1. I examined this question in the paper "Il volontariato tra reciprocità e gratuitá," *Rivista del Volontariato* 1 (1999).

end of the day, what is it that people who establish a helping relationship amongst them are looking for? For the most part, they are trying to create and to consolidate networks of trust—of people who are faithful to each other. It has to be remembered that the Latin origin of the word faithful, *fides,* means a "rope" or "tie" which unites two entities.

Finally, the third reason is that if we reduce volunteering to mere "gratuity," we would no longer know what to rely on to produce relational goods—goods that are real and true inasmuch as they define the well-being of people.[2] As Margalit reminds us, a "decent society" is one whose (economic and social) institutions do not humiliate their members, undermining or negating their human dignity.[3] This is why it is not enough to give—even gratuitously—if it creates *dependency* in the one who receives. What is required is that the act of giving lays down the premise or creates the conditions so that the one who receives is able to express his free determination to stay within the relationship. Allowing those who have received a gift to express their gratitude—in some way and at some time—is equivalent, then, to believing in the freedom of the other. In this way, the gift loses its ambiguities, generating ties of sharing, or rather, of communion.

For these reasons, elsewhere I have written that the principle of reciprocity—which has nothing to do with the principle of exchange of equivalents—is more cogent than the principle of gratuity as a guiding principle enabling us to identify the profound nature of voluntary action.[4] It is more cogent in the sense that the former principle includes the latter one, while the opposite is not true. And yet, such an affirmation gives rise to perplexity and even objections. Why is this? The answer that I find most convincing is that our culture is so caught up in seeing things through an *economistic* lens that when we hear about biunique relations between two or more subjects, we are led to

2. Benedetto Gui has written on the theme of *relational goods.* See Gui, "Interpersonal relations."

3. See Avishai Margalit, *The Decent Society* (Cambridge, Mass.: Harvard University Press, 1998).

4. Stefano Zamagni, "Stato sociale e economia civile: perché é riduttivo parlare di terzo settore," *Quale Stato* 2 (1999).

think that they are relationships based on exchange of equivalents, like the ones which govern usual market relations. In other words, I will give you something or do something for you and straightaway, or in time, you will repay this in money or in some other way. The outcome is that, as fate would have it, we fall into the arms of the skeptics who believe that pure altruism does not exist, since it cannot exist. Nietzsche crystallized this situation when he wrote: "Your neighbor praises the absence of egoism so that he can take advantage of it."

2. Having clarified that point, I will now move on to the first question I posed at the beginning of this paper. To me it seems that the most groundbreaking meaning of the Economy of Communion experience is that it reveals the falseness of the representation of our market societies as insistently hammered into us by the single thought of the "one best way." In brief, it can be summarized in the following way. In traditional societies there are social norms—here understood in the widest sense of the word—which, together with the legal set-up, regulate economic interactions among subjects. In modern societies, on the other hand, the forces of competition prevail and they do so to the extent that they manage to erode the spaces for economic activities governed by conventions and social norms. This representation presupposes that, for this reason, in time the sphere of economic relations will become increasingly regulated by the familiar logic of competition as described in all the economics textbooks. In other words, it is saying that the process of cultural evolution is heading relentlessly toward all interpersonal relationships being caught up in the laws of the market. Naturally, those that promote this idea admit that this substitution can never be complete in the sense that there will always be economic activities that will not be able to be regulated by the rules of the market alone. They are talking about all those activities that are part of the non-profit sector, or rather the "third sector." But this would always constitute a sphere of residual relations, which is of limited quantitative relevance and would therefore have minimal influence on the functional logic of competition.

The consequences of this schizoid representation of economic realities are very serious indeed: the market becomes identified as the ideal type of a place in which those who act are motivated solely by *self-interest*, it does not matter whether it is altruistic or egoistic (As Gary Becker "demonstrates"—as they say—that altruism is nothing other than masked egoism or even illuminated egoism!) From this point onward, the conviction spreads that the only value judgment which the market is capable of making is that of efficiency, understood as a judgment on the adequacy of means in relation to the goal of achieving the greatest possible fulfillment of the interests of those who are participating. In a symmetrical kind of way, there is a concept of the State seen as the ideal type of a place in which collective interests are dominant, and hence, a "public" place dominated by the principle of solidarity.

Well then, the experience of the Economy of Communion contradicts this dichotomous model of social order since it demonstrates, through facts, that it is possible to use the market as a means to manage to reach goals which are by their nature public. More precisely, it is possible to utilize the market not only to produce wealth in an efficient way but also to redistribute it according to some well-defined concept of fairness. It is noticeable that people in our society still believe that the State is the only institution entrusted with the task of redistribution. This idea is so prevalent that redistribution continues to be defined as the principle through which production (of a wealth) is consigned to an authority that has the responsibility of redistributing it, which presupposes the existence of an authority and the separation of tasks between the representatives of this authority and those who have generated production. The Economy of Communion says to us that the market, under a very precise condition, can become an instrument which can reinforce social ties, favoring both the promotion of practices of wealth distribution through its mechanisms (rather than operating outside these or against these) and the creation of an economic space in which it is possible to regenerate those values (such as trust, sympathy, benevolence) on which the existence of the market itself depends.

The condition which I am referring to is that within the market (and hence, not alongside it or outside it), up to the point where the critical mass is reached, a "group" of economic subjects could flourish which have social ties as their original point of reference, and these are lived out through economic activities. Since participation in this activity cannot be separated from the social ties that motivated it, they come under that principle of economic behavior which is the reciprocity principle. The essential aspect of reciprocity, as it is lived in the Economy of Communion, is that transfers cannot be dissociated from human relationships. It is worth saying, that the objects of exchange are not detached from those who create them and hence the exchange that takes place within the market ceases to be anonymous and impersonal.

One could ask: why has dominant economic theory never considered the idea that such an economic space could exist and function? Beyond partisan interests and different kinds of mental dullness, I think that a plausible answer calls into question a double aphorism at its foundation. Firstly, it is not true that—unlike what we continue to read—the preferences that the economic agents seek to maximize on the market have as their exclusive object the goods which enter their choice sets. The way in which the objects are chosen is also relevant, since people attribute value to the possibility of acting—and hence of choosing—on the basis of their moral and religious convictions. It is possible for me to say that option X is superior, on the basis of my preference order, to option Y—for example, since X contains a greater quantity of goods than Y—but if buying X contradicted my personal convictions, which I have gained as a result of my education or previous experiences, then I could decide to buy Y. Taking this into account means rejecting the celebrated precept that "goods are goods," which in the end comes down to the idea that more is better. We know that this is not the case, at least all the times when objects of preference are also *acts of choice* and not simply the things chosen.[5] In fact, it is not irrelevant for the

---

5. See A. Sen, "Maximization and the Act of Choice," *Econometrica*, 65, July 1997.

consumer to know where the goods and services he or she is consuming came from. Neither is it irrelevant for him or her to know the ways in which they were made.

The second error is that of believing that the normative set-up (that is, the juridical norms), culture (that is, the value systems shared by people), and competition (that is, the rules of the market) have to be considered as alternative instruments for solving problems in the social order and, in particular, the coordination of economic decisions. On the contrary, these have to be seen as complementary instruments for the basic reason that if it is true that market transactions depend on social and legal norms prevalent in a certain context, it is also true that the economic process tends to modify endogenously those norms by itself. There is hence a *co-evolution* between effective economic behaviors and changes in the rules of the economic game. It is a co-evolution which official economic science has (almost) never wanted to take into consideration, preferring to postulate—against all empirical evidence—that the success of the market is dependent solely on the egocentrism of those who are part of it. That is tantamount to saying that the market is an institution which is compatible *only* with the egocentric behavior of its actors, while we know that the market is compatible with different cultures. The Economy of Communion is a good demonstration of this.

3. Now I will consider the second question that I indicated at the beginning of this paper. If I have grasped the sign, the formidable challenge which the Economy of Communion poses for orthodox economic science, merely by the fact that it exists at all, can be fully understood if we reflect on the meaning of the famous conjecture put forward by George Stigler, who won the Nobel Prize for Economics and was a co-founder of the famous Chicago School. He wrote: "Allow me, if you will, to predict the result of the systematic and accurate examination of human behavior in situations where self-interest and ethical values are in conflict. Very often, in fact in the great majority of cases, the theory of *self-interest* wins." Now, this conjecture has been widely

proven to be false, as the abundant literature on experimental economics now shows,[6] leaving aside the "mistake" which this passage reveals—contrasting one's own interests with ethical values is the same as admitting that those who defend their own interests are immoral; and yet, the gospel tells us to "Love your neighbor *as* yourself," not "as opposed to yourself."

The scale of the challenge which I have been talking about can be summed up in the following questions. Let's imagine, for the sake of convenience, that only two kinds of actors were at work in the market—those motivated only by *self-interest* and those who practice reciprocity. How would they interact with each other? In the case of voluntary (or private) provisions of public goods, would the interactions of these two kinds of subjects lead to widespread *free riding,* or would the existence of reciprocating agents induce the self-interested ones to act as if they were not self-interested, if only for egocentric reasons?

Secondly, under what circumstances would the reciprocal subjects shape the end result of the economic process—what economists call aggregate equilibrium—and under what conditions would the self-interested ones shape it? For example, we already know that if contracts were always completed, the final result would exhibit properties very similar to those in an economy characterized only by self-interested agents. Whereas when the contracts are not completed—which corresponds to the vast majority of cases in our economies—it is the reciprocating behavior of agents that produces efficient results (*first best solution*).

Thirdly, when different kinds of agents are operating in the market, what role do economic institutions play? It is well known that institutions define the rules of interaction between subjects. Just think of the institutions that overlook the functioning of the labor market, the credit market, business market, and so on. If self-interested and reciprocating actors engage in these markets and if the rules of the game are not, by their

---

6. See, for example, Ernst Fehr and Simon Gachter, "Reciprocity and Economics: The Economic Implications of *Homo Reciprocans,*" *European Economic Review* 42 (1998).

nature, neutral, i.e., indifferent to the motivational structure of individual actors, then we are clearly faced with a problem in the design of economic institutions. For example, should it privilege and favor the economic operation of one kind of actor over another? Since there is no indubitable basis on which to establish whether the anthropological premise of *homo oeconomicus* is worthy of more attention and scientific merit than that of *homo reciprocans,* it is clear that the evolutionary dynamics of a society will depend on the way in which we are able to allow the two forms of economic action to co-exist in the way that we design the institutional framework.

In other words, since the Economy of Communion is based on motivations which are (at least) just as legitimate as the motivation of self-interest, an authentic liberal society cannot block a priori, through a certain institutional structure, the growth and diffusion of the former to the exclusive advantage of the latter, as is happening today. In fact, if effective competition is missing between different actors offering different kinds of goods and, above all, between different ways of interpreting and carrying out economic activities, then citizens see that their freedom has been reduced. Freedom, in fact, cannot be defined only in terms of self-determination—the idea of "free to choose" put forward by Friedman. It has to be seen, above all, in terms of self-fulfillment, that is, the concrete opportunity which every person has to choose his or her own plan of life—including the economic one—in accordance with the values in which he or she believes and to which he or she wants to give witness. Freedom does not only have to take into account the freedom of the other—as individualist liberal thought recognizes—but has to regard the other as a constitutive part of that freedom. The relationship with the other, in fact, is an integral part of freedom, not merely being in relationship with the other.

4. I am coming to the conclusion. Which type of economy does a "decent society" need? In other words, a decent society is one that does not humiliate its citizens by distributing to them, even free of charge, large quantities of goods and services, but at the

same time denying them the possibility of becoming fulfilled. We need an economy in which both these principles—reciprocity and exchange of equivalents—have space to express themselves freely, without those who practice reciprocity feeling that they have to stay in their niche any longer, as if to justify their objection to the historical and natural primacy of self-interest. In his extraordinarily complex behavior, the human person can be guided by a great variety of motivational configurations. The *performance* of a market society, therefore, depends on its capacity to appeal to the "best" individual motivations. It can do this through educating its economic subjects, by means of an epidemiological approach, to seek the greatest well-being for themselves and the other through valuing the practices of social interaction in themselves and not merely as a means to reach individual advantage.

Every piece of research implies responsibilities and risks. In the social sciences, the responsibilities and risks, first and foremost, are moral and political. The economic organization of our Western society is largely based on a well-known economic theory and it uses its scientific status as a source of legitimization. As ever, for better or for worse, science is a guide for action. Therefore, we have to be vigilant. Modern economic science has played its part in the responsibility that legitimized colonialism, exploitative practices, and the generation of new forms of poverty. As paradoxical as it may seem, this has come about while economics has established itself as a science free from value judgments; as a science which, in order to assume the epistemological status of the natural sciences, had to declare that the world of life lays outside the realms of its knowledge. Well, we have to prevent another crime from being committed today: that economic science destroys the hope—above all in young people—that change is possible, since it is within our reach in the economic organization of our societies.[7] The Economy of Communion offers a practical demonstration that it is possible to

---

7. See Luigino Bruni, "Economia e felicitá," L. Fornaciari, ed., *Etica ed economia* (Modena, Italy: University of Modena, 1999).

give without losing and take without taking away, and that this is not only compatible with reason, but is also, under current conditions, the most effective antidote, the most robust bastion against that crime being committed.

✧ Appendix

Complied by Carla Bozzani

Table 1. Geographical Distribution of Economy of Communion Businesses[1]

Italy	246
Western Europe (except Italy)	172
Brazil	82
Eastern Europe	60
Central/Latin America (except Argentina and Brazil)	49
Argentina	45
North America	45
Asia	36
Australia	15
Africa	9
Middle East	2
TOTAL	**761**

1. Data as of September 2001.

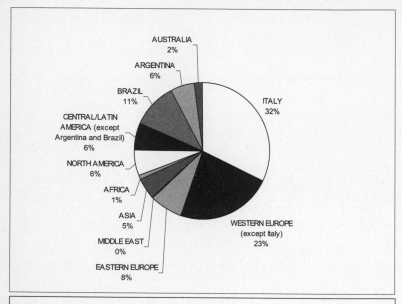

Figure 1: Economy of Communion: Geographical Distribution

Table 2: Breakdown of Sub-Sectors of Business Activities

Commerce	
Clothing	30
Groceries	30
Household	16
Cars	2
Books	7
Photographic materials	1
Information Technology products	4
Healthcare products	13
Various products	58
Total	161
Production	
Clothing	24
Agriculture	29
Food	38
Household goods	16
Various articles	23
Building trade	18
Graphic design	15
Engineering	16
Private healthcare	1
Arts	4
Video productions	3
Various	7
Total	194
Other services	
Consultancy	62
Accounting services	7
Photography	26
Information Technology	26
Legal services	12
Maintenance	18
Medical services	55
Planning services	16
Restoration	5
Education	31
Telephone	1
Electrical services	7
Transport	1
Tourism	12
Various	72
Total	327
TOTAL BUSINESSES	**761**

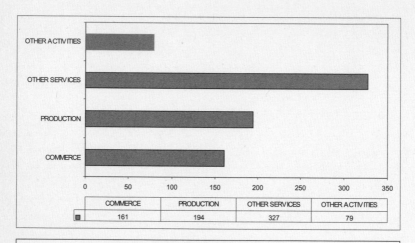

	COMMERCE	PRODUCTION	OTHER SERVICES	OTHER ACTIVITIES
■	161	194	327	79

Figure 2: Economy of Communion: Businesses and Sectors of Activity

Table 3: Number of Employees per Business

less than 50	736
50–100	15
more than 100	10